TOTAL LITERACY CAMPAIGN
PROBLEMS AND PROSPECTS

TOTAL LITERACY CAMPAIGN

Problems and Prospects

By

P. Adinarayana Reddy

ANMOL PUBLICATIONS PVT. LTD.

NEW DELHI - 110 002 (INDIA)

ANMOL PUBLICATIONS PVT. LTD.
4374/4B, Ansari Road, Daryaganj
New Delhi - 110 002
Ph.: 23261597, 23278000
Visit us at: www.anmolpublications.com

Total Literacy Campaign: Problems and Prospects

First Published, 2004

ISBN 81-261-1806-7

PRINTED IN INDIA

Published by J.L. Kumar for Anmol Publications Pvt. Ltd., New Delhi - 110 002 and Printed at Mehra Offset Press, Delhi.

Contents

Preface

Recognising the relationship between literacy and socio-economic development of the country, the National Literacy Mission was established by the Government of India to cover 100 million illiterates by adopting Total Literacy Campaign approach. Under the National Literacy Mission, 428 District Total Literacy Campaigns are functioning in the country. The Chittoor District Total Literacy Campaign is functioning in the name of Akshara Thapasman. The programe has completed the Literacy phase, Post-Literacy programme is organised under Jana Chaityanya Kendras, and the village continuing education centres are being established for the higher order learners. In spite of this, the programme administration has again launched mopping-up of programme to cover all the uncovered, new entrants, dropouts etc. under 100 days literacy programme. In other words the programme could not cover all the target and again it has restarted the entire exercise. Keeping this in view the present study was undertaken to help the administrators to tie up the loose ends of the programme.

The present study was formulated to identify the motives of the participants for attending the Adult Education Centres, causes for their dropout, extent of the participants achievement in Literacy in comparison with school going children and NFE participants, to suggest appropriate entry point for them (multiple entry points) in formal schools and NFE stream, participants attitude towards suitability of IPCL materials, volunteers attitude towards various aspects of the programme in relation to their effectiveness. In addition to the above, it is also intended to probe into the infrastructural facilities available at JCKs, community attitude and support extended for functioning of JCKs, Neo-literates opinion, monitor difficulties and their opinion towards various aspects of the programme was also studied.

The findings of the study will be an eye opener for the field functionaries and administrators to rectify the deficiencies and to replicate the successful experiences and to make it a success. Further based on the findings, the curriculum for the pre-service and in-service training of the field functionaries can be modified by incorporating the various aspects so as to equip the functionaries to the field challenges.

The present report was presented in Six chapters. The Chapter first Introduction briefly narrates the importance of adult literacy, initiation and developments of the TLC of Chittoor district. The Review of Literature forms the Second chapter. The Chapter III presents the Problem and Objectives, Scope of the Study, Limitations etc. The Method of Investigation constitutes Chapter IV of the book. The Chapter V, Analysis and Interpretation of the Data presents the Findings in two sections. Section I shows the Findings relating to the Literacy Phase and Section II presents the findings relating to the post-literacy stage. The last Chapter VI presents Summary and Conclusions of the Study.

The investigator expresses his deep sense of gratitude to the Director, Directorate of Adult Education, Govt. of India for providing financial assistance for undertaking the present study. The investigator also acknowledges the contribution and cooperation provided by Dr. S. Khadar Bhasha, Dr. M. Reddi Bhasha, Sri B. Anand Kumar Reddy, Sri G. Rammana Reddy, Sri G. Reddepa, Smt. Rama Devi and Sri. V. Janaradhana Rao, Research scholars, Dept. of Adult Education, Sri Venkateswara University, Tirupati.

—P.A. Reddy

1

Introduction

Recognising that a socially conscious, vigilant and literate community plays a vital role in a democratic society and also for realization of the objectives of justice, liberty, equality and fraternity, the constitution of India envisaged the provision of approximately eight years of free and compulsory education for all children by 1967. But we are still far away from this goal. The illiteracy, apart from other things, seriously hampers development vital for the advancement of the nation. It is, therefore, highest priority is given in our national planning for the universalisation of elementary education and adult education for the benefit of the out of school children i.e., non-enrollers and drop-outs and the adult illiterates for providing second chance of education and literacy, functionality and awareness respectively at a shortest possible time. Further, National Policy on Education (1986) aims at providing five years of schooling to all those children who attained the age of about 11 years by 1990 or its equivalent through the Non-Formal Stream. Likewise by 1995 all children will be provided free and compulsory education upto 14 years of age.

Further, the New Policy on Education also visualises that adult education would be an appropriate means for reducing economic, social and gender disparities. The principal aim of the New National Programme of Adult Education (NPAE) is to provide education including literacy, to the 80 million illiterates by 1995.

As a result of the new thrust on universalisation of literacy and elementary education, NLM was launched during 1988 to eradicate illiteracy by 1995 in the country and to provide continuing education in a phased manner. As a test case Ernakulam district of Kerala was selected for total eradication of illiteracy. The success of Ernakulam experiment paved the way for selecting more number of districts among the educationally backward states under total literacy programme.

Andhra Pradesh is one of the educationally backward states with 45.11 percent of literacy rate which is less than the national average of 52.11 percent. As on date all the districts are implementing the total literacy programme in A.P. The Chittoor and Hyderabad districts are in forefront in the programme implementation. There were about 6.5 lakhs illiterates in the age group 9 to 35 years in Chittoor district before initiation of the programme. The results of the first phase of the programme shows that about 3.25 lakhs illiterates were made literates. The programme was again restructured to cover the rest of the population and to provide continuing education for the literates, by starting 20,000 Jana Chaitanya Kendras (JCK) throughout the district. Each JCK is manned by two monitors. The functions of the monitors are similar to that of JSN preraks but these monitors are volunteers without any honorarium.

The Chittoor district Total Literacy Campaign 'Akshara Thapasman' also included the children in the age group of 9-14 years as part of target group with the belief that if the out of school children were not taken care, they will continue to be illiterates and objective of total literacy cannot be achieved. Further it is also proposed to help these children to enter into either formal or non-formal stream at an appropriate stage. Hence it is essential to identify the standard of education that they have achieved by participating in Akshara Thapasman Programme and to identify the appropriate stage of formal schooling or the phase of NFE where they can join to continue their education. Further it is also essential to identify the factors affecting their standard of education so that the obstacles can be eliminated and the factors that are promoting their success are strengthened.

The drop-out phenomena is universal to all the educational programmes with varying degrees at various levels. This is also true in the case of total literacy programme. Hence the reasons for their participation in Akshara Thapasman and reasons for drop out from the programme should be identified and this knowledge helps the administrators to strengthen the factors responsible for attracting and retaining the adults and to remove the demotivating factors responsible for the drop-out phenomenon.

The teachers in the total literacy campaign are volunteers who came forward voluntarily to spare some time to teach a small group of 10 illiterates on regular basis. There are about 60,000 volunteers in the district. As the teachers are volunteers, they were from different back-grounds with different experiences. A person with a right attitude towards the work in which he was involved will perform his job effectively. This is also true in the case of volunteers of Akshara Thapasman. Hence, it is necessary to verify the fact by finding out the volunteers attitude and the success achieved by the volunteers in terms of the achievement made by their learners in literacy and awareness. It enables the administrators to identify and to choose those persons who were possessing the qualities required by an effective volunteer and to promote these qualities among the working volunteers through in service training programmes.

The learners success in achieving the required level of competency in literacy and awareness depends on the type of materials that are being used in the programme and the target group. As the programme is meant for eradication of illiteracy, the materials designed are also oriented towards this objective. A specially designed IPCL primers were utilised in the Akshara Thapasman Programme. Hence it is also necessary to see whether the material used in the programme are suitable to its target group which includes children in the age group 9-14 years. The best judges of the suitability of the materials will be the volunteers who were actually used the materials in the programme and also the non-formal education instructors. The opinion of these field functionaries will be highly useful in modification and adaptation of the materials in non-formal education centres of this district and also for other districts. The opinion of the field functionaries, community and participants with regard to the strengths and weaknesses of the programme will help the administration to rectify the deficiencies and to replicate the successful strategies in the other areas.

The Jana Chaitanya Kendras established to promote the literacy and to organise continuing education for neo-literates will play a great role in preventing the neo-literates to relapse into illiteracy.

The Goals and Objectives of the JCK in the Chittoor District are as follows:

- Covering the leftover learners in basic literacy;
- Consolidating and stabilising the literacy skills of neo-literates;
- Upgrading the skills of semi-literates to minimum literacy levels;
- Development of neo-literate books which are suitably graded and adult education oriented;
- Achieving the transition from neo-literacy to autonomous learning through reading materials at increased levels of literacy;
- Striving for autonomous learning among all learners towards creating lifelong learning;
- Consolidating the awareness generated about social issues and to organise people on that basis;
- Providing opportunities for self-development among neo-literates in fields of their choice;
- Establishing institutions for formal/non-formal eduction for continuing education and thereby enriching the learning environment; and
- Identifying and training volunteers who work as agents in these institutions.

Each JCK is staffed by two monitors. The monitors are volunteers working on a non-remunerative basis. Further, they should:

- be settled in life and not looking for opportunities for employment;
- be in the age group of 20-40 years;
- have worked as volunteers in the Akshara Tapasman Programme;
- have passed/failed at least tenth class;
- not belong to any political party;
- have the willingness and ability to organise people; and
- have progressive ideas and be prepared to work on a long-term basis for the education and training of adults.

The monitor in-charge of post-literacy and continuing education should perform the following functions:

- Enabling neo-literates to read fourth primer (Maanava Jeevanam), daily newspapers and fortnightly (Velugubata);
- Helping the dropouts and absentees of the literacy programme to complete the three primers;
- Motivating learners to attend the JCKs;
- Writing the news highlights on the literacy from local newspapers in regional language;
- Providing books (monthlies, weeklies, story books, etc.) to neo-literates supplied by the State Resource Centre for Adult Education, Hyderabad or Zilla Saksharatha Samithi (ZSS), Chittoor;
- Organise simple and short duration training programmes, sports and cultural activities, picnics/visits to government offices and other places;
- Strengthening and utilising the services of village Adult Education Committees for the JCKs;
- Disseminating information on developmental programme and the circulars of ZSS to JCK participants;

- Participating in training programmes, post-literacy campaigns, padayatras, afforestation, family planning, small savings, cleanliness campaigns, review meetings, etc;
- Reporting on the performance of JCKs to ZSS; and
- Helping the non-governmental organisations, agencies and associations with education, training, research and extensions activities;

The monitor of the JCK is the key figure for the successful organisation of JCKs. The opinion of the monitors in terms of the support received from the community, the problems that they have faced in organisation of JCKs and their suggestions in solving the above problems will go a long way in improving the programme.

The second chapter **'Review of Literature'** presents the relevant literature and also the research gaps in the area proposed for the study.

2
Review of Literature

Recognising that the education will bring desirable changes in the adult learners in respect of their knowledge, skills and attitudes in such a way that they may effectively perform changing roles in a changing society, the Govt. of India has launched a number of Adult Education programmes for the benefit of the illiterate adults. A review of the literature on the implementation of various Adult Education programmes launched revealed that a number of research investigations was undertaken both by the individuals and Institutions for not only to identify the loop. holes, bottlenecks, successes but also to replicate the successful aspects and to remove the negative aspects. Further from the available research reports it can be mentioned that of late research in the area of Adult Education is attracting the attention and interest of the research workers and institutions.

Keeping in view of the above an attempt was made to review the available research studies on Current Adult Educational programmes viz. Total Literacy Campaigns and Post-Literacy Campaigns for identifying the gaps in the area of research in Adult Education. The review of the studies was presented in two sections. Section I of the chapter presents the studies relating to the T.L.C's and Section II presents the studies relating to the implementation of P.L.C's.

Section I: Studies relating to Total Literacy Campaigns

Michale Tharakan (1990) evaluated the Eranakulum District TLC and found that the people centred propaganda measures like jathas were more effective than the mediacentred propaganda interventions.

Denzil Saldanha (1992) evaluated the literacy campaign of Sindu Durg. The major finding of the study reveals that the vast majority (82%) of the enrolled learners in the age group of 15-35 years performed better than those aged in 36-60 years in literacy.

Anil Bhatt (1993) evaluated the Tumkur District literacy campaign and found that 71.5% of the sample were able to attained 50% of markers in each of the 3 segments of literacy viz. reading, writing and arithmetic. In addition to the above, over. 90% of adult learners tested, scored the minimum marks of 50% in reading and numeracy. However writing was found to be critical skill and most difficult to develop. The performance of the children in the age group of 9-14 was better (79-2%) than the age group of 15-35 years (77.5%). The performance of the persons who were working was found to be better than those who were not working. Further, the study also disclosed that the performance of males over females and STs over SCs were found to be better.

Bh. Krishnamurthy and others (1993) evaluated the total literacy campaign of Chittoor district. The major findings of the study are as follows.

1. The literacy attainment of the target population of 9-35 years is 64.3 per cent as per the NLM norms.
2. The TLC in Chittoor has resulted in raising the literacy level among 9-35 years to 86.70 per cent.
3. Majority of the participants of the TLC belongs to SC, ST and BC sections.
4. The composition of the selected sample shows that majority of the sample constitutes women and agricultural labour.
5. Only 12.7 percent of the selected sample had some earlier schooling.

6. The performance of the sample disclosed that 78 percent of the sample gained A-K grades. The caste-wise analysis shows that over 80 percent of SCs. 79% of OC, 78% of STs and 74% of BC's obtained grades between A-C. The female learners have fared better than male learners. The achievement of literacy by the sample shows that 64.3 percent reached the prescribed level of literacy. The study also suggested that the reading material must be designed scientifically associating a linguist with the preparation of primers.

Denzil Saldanha (1992) while evaluating the TLC of Wardha District found that 76.2% of the learners attained 60% marks. The major difficulties of the learners in the language are the problems of joint letter writing as compared to Reading and expressing one self creatively in a given format for example the letter writing. Sex of the instructor appeared to influence the performance of the learner and an instructor of the same sex has an effect on the performance of the learners.

Mustaq Ahamad and others (1992) evaluated the TLC of Midnapore District and reported that 77.6% of the sample learners were found to have attained the NLM norms. Numeracy skills of the learners were more developed and writing skills were weakest. Adult learners performed better than NFE group learners. Performance of male learners was better than the female earners. Learners with some previous formal schooling background even if rudimentary, performed slightly better than those who never attended any formal school. IPCL primers appear to be more effective than Non IPCL Primers.

Gopalakrishna Reddy (1993) evaluated the literacy campaign of Vishakhapatnam District with the objective of not only to assess the performance of the learners but also to study the level of awareness, impact of the programme and to identify the drawbacks in implementation of the programme. The findings of the study shows that over 96.61% of the sample expressed satisfaction in functioning of the programme and 81.4% felt that the programme is making good efforts in imparting literacy to the non-literates in the district. Participation of the learners in the development programmes of the village was found to be impressive. Family welfare and immunisation programmes have been accepted by the people of all the villages. The parents realised the importance of the education and re-enrolled all their children in the formal schools. The Anti-Arrack movement was the result of the growth of literacy and awareness among the women which ultimately brought-out pressure on the government to introduce prohibition in the state of A.P.

Shastry and Chariyulu (1993) evaluated the literacy campaign of West Godavari District of A.P. and found that (81.79%) of the sample learners passed the literacy test. The success rate of male and female is almost equal.

Council for social development (1993) conducted on external evaluation of Karimnagar District literacy campaign with an objective to evaluate achievement levels of learners in five main component of literacy viz. ability to read, write, identify symbols, simple mathematical calculations and to sign. The findings of the study discloses that 92.3% of sample learners have become neo-literates. The achievement rate of the learners below 15 years of age group was 92% and above 35 years age group was 88%. The Gender and caste did not make any significant difference in terms of achievement levels. However age seems to have some impact on achievement levels as the youngest people show better performance than the older ones. The study also revealed that presence of facilities like irrigation, bank, post office, motorable road, etc did not have any impact on achievement levels. Villages with less facilities reported high percentage of achievement indicating the commitment and vigour of the volunteers, officials and other functionaries involved in the programme.

The Institute of Social Science (1993) found that only 18.2% of the sample were able to attained the NLM norm of literacy in the total literacy campaign of Goa. Further the obtained mean achievement marks revealed that male and female have obtained 41.5% and 27.8% respectively.

Indradeva (1993) evaluated the TLC of Bilaspur District.

The findings of the study shows that 74% of the learners reached the NLM norms. The average score secured by the successful learner in reading, writing and numeracy were 81.66 and 87 per cent respectively.

The evaluation of Jalna District conducted by the Deshpande (1993) revealed that an over all 88% of the sample learners achieved NLM norms. More or less men and women secured equal percentage. The performance of the learners in the age group of 9-14 years were found to be good and in some cases little better than the adult learners. The study also revealed that the learners have secured low mean scores in writing ability in comparison with reading and numeracy.

Sardar Patel Institute of Economic and Social Research (1993) evaluated the Kheda District literacy campaign. The study revealed that 86.2% of the learners were successful in literacy. With regard to the awareness aspects, the learners are aware of personal cleanliness (97.7%), aware of immunisation programme (45.6), family programme (58.11), keeping the house and surroundings clean (56.55%) etc. In addition, the sample is also aware of development and economic aspect (87.16%), social aspects like dowry system, social evils, minimum age of knowledge, removal of untouchability, family planning (78%) etc.

Tribal and Harijan Research cum Training Institute, (1993) evaluated the literacy campaign of Sundergarh District. The findings of the study shows that 59 percent of the sample have attained 70% of marks. The enquiry with regard to the non-attendance of learners revealed that stiff course of study (15.14%), Lack of proper teaching procedure (16.29%) and Socio-economic and personal constrain (22.95%) are the major causes.

Tata Institute of Social Science (1993) evaluated the TLC of Pune and found that 76.91% of the sample learners were found to be successful as per the NLM norms. The percentage of achievement of the females was 75.55% which is slightly more than the males (75.39). The letter writing was weakest ability among the literates.

Tata Institute of Social Science (1993) evaluated the TLC of Latur District. The finding of the study shows that about 82% of the evaluated learners scored above 50% marks in literacy test but only 49.7% reached the NLM norm of literacy. As per NLM norm 58.4% of the males and 55.2% of females succeeded the test. The performance of three components of literacy shows that the mean performance is better in numeracy than reading and writing.

The Tata Institute of social sciences (1993) while evaluating the Nanded total literacy campaign found that only 42% the learners have reached the NLM norm in literacy. The findings also revealed that those who had less than 6 months of learning performed poor in literacy compared to those who had more than 6 months of instructions.

Gokul O. Parekh (1994) evaluated the Vadodara District literacy campaign and found that the literacy campaign focused emphasis on imparting the 3 Rs. It is understood that campaign has succeeded in arousing awareness about the various issues touching the lives of the neo-literates. The volunteer factors along-with tight monitoring and control of the campaigns seems to have brought about considerable importance in the literacy scenario in the District. The propaganda, publicity, Training and actual teaching work has contributed a lot for the success of the campaign.

Centre for media Studies (1994) conducted a pilot study for evaluating he literacy campaign of Panipat of Haryana state. The findings reveals that 1/3 of the sample has achieved 70% of marks. The female learners performed better than the male. The achievement of the adults was better than the children in the age group of 9-14 years. The target performance in writing is 20.9% and the achievement in other two components i.e., reading and numeracy is double than the writing.

Karve Institute of social services (1994) has evaluated the literacy campaign of Parbhani District of Maharastra. The outcome of the study reveals that about 57% of the sample of the study were found to be attained the NLM norms in the literacy. However 63.48% evaluated learners scored 70% and above. It also reveals that those who scored 70% aggregate could not achieve 50% in writing ability. Further majority of learners felt very difficult in the component of essay writing which obviously is not so-much a part of the villager life in the rural areas.

Mustaq Ahmad (1994) evaluated the total literacy campaign of Almora and found that only 40.03% of the learners could reach the NLM norms in literacy.

Shantha Mohan (1994) evaluated the literacy campaign of Dakshina Kannada and found that the skill to read was found to be very high in all the cases and the skill to write was very weak. However learners with less than 25 years were able to write better than the those belonging to the older age group.

Paul Valiakanadathil and Saravanan (1993) evaluated the literacy campaign of Mandya District. The out-come of the evaluation revealed that 77.4% have achieved NLM norms in literacy. The success rate of males was higher than the females. The learners belongs to SC/ST have also reached on-par with other category of learners in literacy performance. The performance of lower age group 9-14 years was lower than the 15-35 age group. The writing skill was found to be very weak.

Kishore Attavar (1994) evaluated the Shimoga District literacy campaign and found half of the learners tested has achieved NLM norm in literacy. The comparative performance of the men and women revealed that men has scored more than women, age-wise achievements shows that the children in the age group of 9-14 years has scored better (52.38%) than the 15-35 age group (50.30%). The ST sample has fared better (75.83) than the SC sample (55.55%). With regard to the achievement in various literacy abilities, 80.41% of learners in reading, 79.37% in numeracy and 42.70% in writing ability attained 50% or more marks.

Om Mehta (1994) evaluated the literacy campaign of Durg District of Madya Pradesh and the findings are as follows. Eighty percent of the rural learners and 72.01% of the learners achieved the literacy according to NLM norms. Over 90% of the SC/ST and BC participated learners have achieved the literacy. The programme of environment building was very effective and was mainly based on wall writing, kala jatha, local jatha etc.

Sardar Patel Institute of Economic and Social Research (1994) evaluated the literacy campaign of Dang District of Gujarath. Thee findings of the study shows that 62% of the sample learners secured 50% of marks in aggregate and only 23.93% secured 70% marks in aggregate. The outcome of male learners was better than the females and 66% Scheduled Tribes have scored more that 50%. On the other hand only around 33% each belonging to SC, Bakshi panch and others have secured 50% and more. Occupation-wise 80% labourers have secured more than 50% of the marks.

Sardar Patel Institute of Economic and Social Research (1994) evaluated the literacy campaign of Sunder Nagar District literacy campaign. The study shows that more than 86% of neo literates scored 50% marks and only 22% secured 70% and above marks in literacy test. The achievement in reading, writing and numeracy was found to be 83%, 62% and 88% respectively.

Sardar Patel Institute of Economics and Social Research (1993) evaluated the literacy campaign of Ahmadabad and assessed the achievement as well-as the impact of the camaign. The results of the study disclosed that 83.15% of the sample learners were declared successful. It also reveals that the relation between social caste and literacy out-comes displayed better in a major out comes of the literacy campaign. The relatively better performance of these groups are in the areas of Health, Hygiene, Social and Economic awareness.

Sardar Patel Institute of Economics and Social Research (1993) assessed the impact of literacy campaign of Bhava Nagar city on three aspects i.e., Health, Social and Environmental awareness. The results indicated that 50 60% of the neo-iterates were aware of the Health and Hygiene, with regards to social awareness fifty percent of the sample neo-literates reported increase in social awareness in the selected areas. Environmental awareness point of view, 63 per cent of the neo-literates recognised the importance of the conservation of environment and the impact of environment on social life, tree plantation, use of forest products etc.

Sidda Gowda (1996) evaluated the "Akshara Vani" of Chitra

Durga District and found that 32.97% of the Neo-literates have scored 70%. Numeracy is found to be easiest skill (71.06%) followed by reading (66.4%) and writing (44.06%). The men and women learners have performed equally. Christian neo-literates fared better in test than the other religious groups. There is no visible differences in the performance between different caste groups. Occupation wise neo-literates belonging to agriculture stood first with 40.82% followed by House wives (38.83%), Labourers (36.61%) and others (33.39%). Income wise high income group fared well. A large number of dropouts occurred due to learners work load for livelihood and other personal problems.

The review of the above studies relating to the TLC clearly shows that the majority of the studies related to the evaluation of the literacy out-comes only. Except very few, no investigation was aimed to identify the motives, causes for drop-outs, comparative performance of the TLC, with NFE and Formal school children, attitudes and effectiveness of the functionaries etc. Hence there is a need to take up a comprehensive study to evaluate a various factors involved in the implementation of the programmes.

Section II: Studies Relating to the Post-literacy Programmes

The studies relating to the implementation of post-literacy programmes and its components are reviewed. The studies are as follows.

Nair, Omanna and Rehim (1992) studied the functioning of J.S.Ns. under N.Y.K. of Kerala. The study revealed that preraks were drawn from both the sexs equally, in the age group of 9-20 years, with annual income ranges from Rs. 1000 to 2000 and half of them belong to backward communities.

It also disclosed that the preraks had adequate experience in literacy programmes and affiliated to some cultural and sport organisations. The interest in social work prompted them to join as preraks with regard to the physical facilities. One third of them were having improvised teaching aids half of them had separate reading room and none of them having own building.

The major sources for learning materials were found to be N.Y.Ks and all of them were receiving news papers. The drop-Outs, inadequate training and funds were the major problem of the J.S.N.

Vasumathi (1992) studied the functioning of Jana Sikshana Nilayamas in Kannur District of Kerala and found that majority of the users belongs to neo-literates especially womens. All the J.S.Ns are having building with sufficient furnitures, separate room for reading and all the J.S.Ns are electrified. The background of the preraks reveals that majority of them had up to 5 years of experience in adult education and affiliated to some cultural or sports clubs. All the J.S.Ns have organised various cultural and co-curricular activities such as Literacy Jathas, Street dramas, Meetings, Awareness Campaigns, Study tours to governmental departments. Un-interested neo-literates, Inadequate learning materials, lack of public support, lack of physical facilities and play ground were found to be major problems encountered by the J.S.Ns in organising its activities.

Muthuchamy (1992) identify the discrepancy between the ideal performance and actual performance of the preraks in their roles as organiser of literacy/post literacy activities (56.25), generator of awareness (62.60), organiser of cultural and recreational programmes (56%), mobiliser of resources (60.64%), recorder of educational activities (35.20%), professional devotion (61.20%), guidance activity (65.86%) and supervisory functions, (38.88%). The study also identified the problems of the preraks in their role performance.

Adhilakshmi (1993) found that the J.S.N. were confined to post literacy activities alone and none of them were having A.V. facilities. It is also identified that the performance of J.S.Ns manned by different age and experience groups were found to be similar.

Reddappa (1993) identified that women, forward caste, agricultural background, more income, more educated married, elders, more positive attitude were found to be determinants of effective preraks.

Directorate of Adult Education (1994) evaluated the functioning of the scheme of J.S.Ns for highlighting the strengths and suggestions for over come the existing deficiencies. The findings of the study shows that it has positive impact on rural population. The provision of J.S.N. facilities has succeed in enhancing the demand for education particularly continuing education it is operated with high participation levels. The need for grass-root level institutions catering to continuing education is being actually felt in post literacy and total literacy campaign districts.

State resource centre of Karnataka (1995) while conducting an observational study on J.S.Ns found that majority of J.S.Ns were functioned for a few hours in a day. Most of the J.S.Ns were not provided with job related literature and the available reading materials were kept ideal and there is no evidence for cultural and sports activities. The facilities provided in the J.S.Ns, the physical facilities and equipment provided to J.S.N. either missing or misused. The money intended for preraks salary and other J.S.N. activities were not paid in time. Majority of the J.S.Ns were not having their own building and J.S.Ns were not given any role in education for all programme in Total Literacy Campaign in the state.

Padmanabaiah and Kumaraswamy (1995) identified the problems faced by the monitors in organising Jana Chaithanya Kendra for providing post-literacy and continuing education for neo-literates.

P.A. Reddy (1996) studied the functioning of J.S.Ns in Chittoor district and found that all most all the J.S.N. have poor housing facilities and does not have adequate furniture and book keeping facilities. Caste of the preraks were found to be closely associated with their effectiveness. The reading material supplied to the J.S.N. and reading interest of the neo-literates were found to be closely associated. Further the association between preraks attitude and effectiveness is closely associated with performance of the J.S.Ns. The community support and attitude towards J.S.N. has an effect on their performance.

Janardhana Rao V. (1996) enquired in problems faced in

Jana Chaithanya Kendras. The findings of the study revealed that lack of suitable materials, place for J.C.K. co-operation of experts, village leaders, motivation among neo-literates were found to be prominent problems. In addition to the above availability of young and inexperienced monitors involvement of caste religion and village politics and fractions were also found to be affecting the performance of the J.C.Ks.

Mohanty and Prusty (1996) identified the items location of the centre, lack of infrastructure, No T.V & Radio, untimely supply of teaching learning materials, corruption and mal—practice in supervision, lack of local people support in organising J.S.N. activities and lack of effective training and functionaries as major problems in organising the J.S.Ns.

The review of the above studies show that the attempts made by the investigators mostly aimed to identify the literacy out comes of the adult participants of the T.L.Cs and very few have made attempt on other factors relating to the programme. Further the review on P.L.Cs also shows that the attempts are of very narrow in its scope covering only few aspects. Practically there was no attempt to evaluate the programme comprehensively covering the important aspects of literacy and post-literacy programme. Keeping in view of the above the present attempt was made to evaluate the T.L.C. of Chittoor district covering all phases viz. literacy and post-literacy and various aspects involved from pre-launching to post-literacy stage.

The Chapter III statement of the problem presents the problem to be investigated, scope of the study, need of the study, objectives of the study and limitations of the study.

3

Statement of the Problem and Objectives of the Study

The chapter describes the statement of the problem, need of the study, objectives of the study and limitations of the study etc.

Statement of the Problem

A Study of the certain aspects of the Akshara Thapasman Programme (Total Literacy Campaign) of Chittoor District, A.P.

Scope of the Study

The scope of the present study is very wide as the aspects planned to cover are varied and numerous. However broadly speaking, the present investigation intended to identify the motives of the participants for attending the ATP centres, causes for the drop-outs, functionaries opinion towards the suitability of the learning materials, extent of literacy achieved by the learners, volunteers attitude and their effectiveness. In addition to the above, study is also intended to cover the aspects relating to the post-literacy programme viz., availability of infrastructure for post--literacy centre, community attitude and support to the JCKs, monitors problems, field functionaries opinion towards JCK, finally performance of JCKs in terms of the various roles to be performed by them etc.

Need of the Study

The government of India has launched a National Literacy Mission to accelerate the socio-economic development of the country by qualifying vast masses of the human resources not only by promoting literacy but also the social consciousness and functionality. In order to realise the above, NLM sponsored the total literacy campaigns in thee selected districts. The Chittoor district of A.P. is on of the first phase districts to implement TLC in the name of Aakshra Thapasman Programme (ATP). Now the programme is in the third phase i.e., it is in the process of establishing continuing education centres. However inspite of its success in literacy and post-literacy fronts, still it is consolidating its gains and rectifying the deficiencies. As a result of this, the moping-up of the programme was conceived to cover the left overs and drop-outs through 100 days literacy programme. Post-literacy programme is in operation in the form of Janachaityanya Kendras. The continuing education centres are being established for the higher order learners. In view of its operation in three stages, there is a need to identify why the participants joined the programme and also left. Is it the distributed material is not attractive? The volunteers are not effective or indifferent ? What infrastructure is available? and extent of its usefulness. The post-literacy centres are managed by monitors. The role of monitor is divergent and is responsible not only for promotion of literacy but also to make it consolidated. In this process, monitor has to encounter a number of problems. The effectiveness of the jana Chaitanya Kendras are largely depends on the performance of the monitors and the community support received by them. As the field functionaries are drawn from various walks of life, they should be thoroughly trained not only to equip them with required skills and knowledge but also to act a change agents. The programme will be successful only if all the aspects of the system performs well or otherwise the investment made interms of man-hours, money, material will go a waste. Hence, keeping inview of the above, the present study was formulated with the following objectives.

(i) Objectives

1. To find out the motives of the participants for attending the Akshara Thapasman Programme.
2. To find out the reasons for dropping out from the Akshara Thapasman Centres.

3. To study the suitability of learning materials used in the Akshara Thapasman Centres.
4. To assess the standard of education received by the participants in Akshara Thapasman Programme.
5. To suggest appropriate entry point into the system of formal education and non-formal education programme to the participants of the Akshara Thapasman Programme.
6. To study the relationship between volunteers attitude towards Akshara Thapasman Programme and their effectiveness in terms of the participants' achievement in literacy.
7. To find out the availability of the infrastructure for the organisation of Jana Chaitanya Kendras.
8. To assess the community attitude towards the functioning of jana Chaitanya Kendras.
9. To assess the community support received by the monitors for effective organisation of Jana Chaityanya Kendras.
10. To find out the neo-literates' attitude towards the functioning of Jana Chaitanya kendras.
11. To identify the problems of the monitors in implementation of the Jana Chaitanya Kendras.
12. To assess the performance of monitor of JCKs.
13. To ascertain the opinion of the field functionaries viz., Mandal Coordinators, Village Coordinators, Volunteers, JCK monitors with regard to
    - Training
    - Monitoring
    - Evaluation
    - Strengths of the programme
    - Deficiencies of the programme and
    - Suggestions for improving the quality of the programme.

Limitations of the Study

- The study attempts to cover a number of factors at a time and as a result the depth of the aspects may not be much.
- The study is limited to TLC & PLCs of Chittoor district only.
- The study was limited to the selected sample of the areas chosen for the study and
- Impact of the literacy on the target was not attempted.

4

Method of Investigation

The aim of the study is to identify the motives of the participants, causes of drop-outs, attitude of functionaries, Learners performance in literacy and Functionaries, Monitor effectiveness, Community support, opinion of the community and neo-literates towards the functioning of the J.C.Ks, Problems of the monitors and opinion of the field functionaries towards various aspects of the programme etc. In order to generate the data on the various aspects mentioned above requires various tools. A review of tools available on the above aspects revealed that, the available tools are not suitable to the present study as the tools are developed for different purposes on different cliental on different programmes. Hence the investigator developed the following tools.

1. A scale to identify the learners motives for attending Akshara Thapasman Centres.
2. A scale to identify the reasons for drop-out from Akshara Thapasman centres.
3. A scale to measure the suitability of learning materials.
4. A scale to measure volunteers attitude towards Akshara Thapasman programme.
5. An achievement test to measure 3 R's and awareness.
6. A questionaire to measure the performance of JCK.
7. A scale to measure community attitude towards JCK.

8. A scale to measure Community Support towards JCK.
9. A rating scale to identify the problems of the monitors.
10. A scale to measure neo-literate attitudes towards JCK.
11. A scale to measure monitor effectiveness.
12. A scale to measure the field functionaries attitude towards effectiveness of training, monitoring and evaluation.

Procedure Adopted for the Development of the Tools

As a first step in the process of development of the tools, the investigator has consulted the field functionaries, learners, community and experts in the field to generate a list of items to be included in the tool to be developed. Again this list of the items were supplemented through the review of literature. The list thus developed was presented to a panel of five experts in the field of Adult Education with a request to go through the items and suggest for modification; removal of ambiguous items and to add relevant items. The suggestions of the experts were carried out. The tools thus developed have two sections, Section I represent the personal information of the sample and Section II consisted of the items relating to the aspect to be measure.

Scoring Procedure of the Tool

Keeping inview of the area, sample and the suggestions of the experts, suitable scoring/rating procedure was evolved to score the individuals performance on the particular aspect. For example numerical rating procedure was adopted in case of identifying the motives, causes for drop-outs, opinion towards the suitability of the learning materials, volunteers attitude towards A.T.P., Field functionaries and neo-literates opinion on the functioning of J.C.Ks. etc. For measuring the learners achievement in literacy a different approach of awarding scores was adopted.

Pilot Study

The tools thus developed was administered to a randomly selected sample of 100 from the study area. Before administering the tools the investigator has explained the method of filling the tools. Care was also taken to see that the sample drawn should represent all the strata of the society.

Scoring of the Items

The items of the tools were scored according to the procedure laid down by the investigator for example incase of the attitude scales numerical values of 1, 2, 3, 4 & 5, for positive items and 5, 4, 3, 2 and 1 for negative items was adopted for the descriptive cues.

Selection of Items

Based on the scores obtained, schedules/scales were arranged in descending order. The top 27 and bottom 27 i.e., 27 percent were chosen to find-out the discriminative value, usefulness of the item and difficulty level of the items were calculated between these two groups and the items with less than prescribed values (t, value and discriminative value) were discarded and all those items having more than the prescribed level were retained for the final form of the tool. The above common procedure was adopted for developing the tools required for the study.

Reliability and Validity

The reliability of the above tools were established by using test-retest reliability method. The tools were found to be highly reliable. Further the validity of the tools were also established through content, item and instrensic validity. The tools were found to be highly valid.

Study Area and Sample

The present study was aimed to study the functioning of Total literacy Campaign of Chittoor district with reference to Literacy and Post-Literacy phase. Hence the Chittoor district forms the locale of the study.

Sample

For the purpose of the present study different types of respondents viz., Akshara Thapasman participants, drop-outs volunteers and others functionaries of the programme, NFE instructors, JCK monitors, neo-literates, and community are required to be consulted for collecting relevant data. The size of the sample of the different groups and mode of selections are given below.

The Chittoor district consists of 66 Revenue Mandals. For selecting the sample for the present study, eleven Mandals out of the list of 66 Mandals i.e., every 6th Mandal were selected randomly by following systematic sampling ,techniques in the first stage. There would be around 300 villages in these 11 Mandals. In the second stage, out of 300 villages a sample of 60 villages was selected randomly by choosing not less than 5 villages from each Mandal for selecting various types of samples required for the study.

Out of 60 villages selected, 600 Akshara Thapasman participants and 200 drop outs were selected randomly by choosing not less than 10 participants and 5 dropouts respectively from each village for obtaining the motives of the participants and causes for drop-outs.

200 volunteers was selected randomly from among the volunteers working in these 60 villages to gather their opinion about the suitability of the materials used, to measure their attitude towards Akshara Thapasman programme and to ascertain about their opinion on certain issues of the programme. Further, 200 NEF teachers were selected from these villages to gather their opinion about the suitability of the materials used in the programme to all the participants belonging to different age groups.

There are about 3300 functionaries of the programme at various levels viz., village, Mandal and district levels. 200 functionaries were selected randomly to obtain their opinions about the various issues of the programme.

Apart from the above, 200 neo-literats, 200 community representatives, 200 JCK monitors were also selected from the 60 villages randomly for collecting relevant data from them. In brief, the various categories of the sample selected are as follows:

1.	Akshara Thapasman participants	600
2.	Akshara Thapasman drop-outs	200
3.	Akshara Thapasman volunteers	200
4.	Non-formal education instructors	200
5.	Akshara Thapasman functionaries	200
6.	Neo-literats	200
7.	Community representatives	200
8.	JCK monitories	200

Data Collection and Analysis

The tools thus developed was administered to the selected sample separately and the data was pooled and analysed by using appropriate statistical techniques.

The next chapter data Analysis and findings of the study will present the findings in two sections. The Section A shows the results obtained in the literacy phase and Section B presents the various aspects relations to the functioning of Post-literacy programme.

5

Analysis and Interpretation of the Data

The findings of the study and its implications are presented in this chapter under two Sections A & B. Section A Present the information relating to the literacy phase and Section B present the findings relating to the Post-literacy phase.

Section A of the Chapter presents the findings in five units. Unit I present the motives of the participants of the ATP. Unit II identifies the causes for drop-outs. The findings of the suitability of learning materials were presented in the Units III. Unit IV throws light on the literacy achievement of the learners and also discloses the appropriate entry point into the system of formal education, Non-Formal education Programme. The Unit V reveals the relationship between volunteers attitude towards ATP and their effectiveness. The Section B, of the chapter present the findings of the study relating to the functioning of the JCKs in nine units. Unit I of the section shows the infrastructure available for organisation of J.C.K. activities. Unit II describes the community attitude towards the functioning of the J.C.Ks, and the community support received by the monitors for effective organisation of J.C.Ks. was discussed in Unit III. In Unit IV shows the neo-literates opinion towards various activities of the J.C.Ks and probable strategies were formulated for over coming the above problems. The Unit VII of the chapter presence the performance of the monitors of the J.C.K. The field functionaries opinion on various aspects of the programme VIZ training, Monitoring, Evaluation was presented in Unit VIII, Strength and Deficiencies, Suggestions for improve of the programme was presented in the Unit IX.

SECTION—A

PERFORMANCE OF THE LITERACY PHASE OF THE AKSHARA THAPASMAN PROGRAMME

Unit I: Motive of the Participants

The participants of the programme may be attending the adult education centres with different intentions and to satisfy their urge for learning. The centre activities will be successful only if the centre is capable of catering to the needs of the participants. The need satisfaction will prompt for higher enrolment, retention of the adults and active participation of the community in the A.T.P. Centres. Further identification of the motives of the participants is a pre-condition to formulate the curricular contents to modify the existing teaching learning materials and to enhance the quality of the teaching and learning activites. Keeping this in view, the motives of the participants were identified and also classified into three groups based on the criterion mean motive score $\pm$ 1/2 S.D. viz. More popular motives, Popular motives and Less popular motives. Out of the 63 items, 16 were categorised as more popular, 31 as popular and 16 of them as less popular motives. The classification reveals that 3/4 of the listed items were found to be popular among the participants. In other-wards majority of the adults were attending the centres with different motives. Hence it is the duty of the field functionaries to satisfy the participants by providing the suitable information either orally or in the form of small booklets written in easy language. The motives identified as popular belongs to the areas of literacy awareness and to some extent relates to development aspects like health Agriculture, Enviorment etc. The programme administration should take note of the above and the publishers of the Post-literacy materials, Public relation office,

Development departments should be advised to produce more materials on the above aspects and may be disseminated widely for the benefit of the community as a whole.

The following pages will provide more details about the nature of motives of participants for attending adult education centres.

(i) More Popular Motives

From the Table 1 it is evident that out of 63 motives, 16 motives were found to be more popular motives. The nature of the motives rated as more popular discloses that the participants has chosen to attend the centres to learn the literacy, ways and means of applying it in their day to day life. Some of the items chosen related to awareness aspects. Probably the target might have faced the situations where these aspects should have come across in their day to day life. Further the adults also checked developmental issues as their motives for attending the ATP Centres. The above clearly discloses that the target are selective in their motives for attending the ATPCentres. Hence it is necessary to satisfy the participants motives by providing opportunities for promoting literacy and by providing information on awareness and developmental aspects. The above action not only help the target to learn what they want but also act as motivators for attracting more number of their peer group to get enroll and to attend regularly to the ATP Centres.

Table 1

More Popular Motives and Respective Mean Values

S.No.	*More Popular Motives*	*Mean*
1.	Read Newspapers	4.09
2.	To know more about the social evils	3.95
3.	To know how men and women are equal in all aspects	3.94
4.	To know government subsidies and loan facilities	3.93

Contd.

Table Contd.

S.No.	*More Popular Motives*	*Mean*
5.	To understand the rights and duties of a citizen in democracy	3.92
6.	To maintain domestic accounts	3.85
7.	To know the prices of the essential goods	3.85
8.	Learn to read and write	3.84
9.	To understand the content of the nutritious and balanced diet	3.84
10.	Learn to read letters	3.83
11.	To learn to sign	3.83
12.	To know the ways and means of improving family economic status	3.81
13.	To learn to calculate daily wages	3.80
14.	To learn new and good habits from others	3.78
15.	To know the methods of preservation of food	3.76
16.	To know the better utility of right for voting	3.75

(ii) Popular Motives

The Table 2 shows the items checked as popular motives. Out of 63 motives, 32 motives were found to be popular motives i.e. half of the items included in the scale. In other words the selected sample has given second priority to the half of the items. The items chosen relates to the areas of further education, awareness, health, development, environment, agriculture etc. It clearly demonstrates that the motives are of multidimensional and relates to their day to day life. Hence it is necessary to stress on the above aspects in the course of promotion of literacy. Further the above aspects should be kept in mind while preparing the post-literacy materials.

Table 2

Popular Motives and Respective Mean Values

S. No.	*Popular Motives*	*Means*
1.	To know more about the life insurance corporation schemes	3.74
2.	To know about common diseases of the children and their prevention	3.72
3.	To learn from others	3.71
4.	To know about the government sponsored developmental schemes	3.69
5.	To know about pregnant women care	3.69
6.	To understand the day to day problems	3.68
7.	To know about the environmental pollution and its prevention.	3.66
8.	To solve the problems raised by the children as a parent	3.66
9.	To know different methods of safe family planning methods	3.64
10.	Read name plates on the buses	3.62
11.	Methods of utilising leisure time profitably	3.62
12.	To know government social welfare programme	3.61
13.	To know laws and rights	3.61
14.	To know different and suitable occupational skills for women	3.59
15.	To know the govt. health and developmental schemes	3.57

Contd.

Table Contd.

S. No.	*Popular Motives*	*Means*
16.	To promote community integration by meeting other regularly	3.57
17.	Read the labels on the fertiliser bags and to know their composition	3.54
18.	To know about the children education and type of facilities to be provided to them	3.53
19.	Strong desire for education	3.53
20.	To learn new methods of agriculture	3.51
21.	To maintain accounts of the agriculture	3.50
22.	To know about the high yielding varieties of mango and coconut	3.48
23.	To study further	3.47
24.	To learn to improve family health and income through kitchen garden	3.47
25.	To know about the growing of gardens which will be yielding more income	3.46
26.	To utilise the developmental programme by knowing them	3.44
27.	To know the programmes taken-up for the socio economic development of the backwards	3.39
28.	To know more about the social forestry scheme	3.37
29.	To improve the occupational skills	3.35
30.	To know methods of obtaining fertilisers, seeds and loans from single windows	3.35
31.	Read stories and novels	3.34

(iii) Less Popular Motives

Table 3 depicts the less popular motives of the adults for attending the ATP Centres. Out of 63 items presented to the sample, 16 were checked as less popular motives. Though these motives were found to be less popular, they should not be ignored as the mean motive score shows that the items were also popular and belongs to agriculture, animal husbandry and awareness. It is true that the sample of the study were already engaged in agriculture and subsidiary occupations like animals husbandry as most of the sample are drawn from rural population who depends on the above for their lively hood. Hence it is necessary to upgrade their skills in the above and to help them to perform their activities in a more effective manner.

Table 3

Less Popular Motives and their Respective Means Values

S. No.	*Less Popular Motives*	*Means*
1.	To know the different methods of storage of grains	3.33
2.	To know the problems of the agricultural labourers	3.33
3.	To know about worldly affairs	3.32
4.	To know about the high yielding subsidiary occupations	3.32
5.	To know the different diseases attacking different crops and their prevention	3.31
6.	To know the methods of safe-gardening the corps from animals, birds and especially from rats	3.28
7.	To know about the problems to be arised due to fractions and groups politics	3.27
8.	To know different varieties of cattles yielding more milk	3.26

Contd.

Table Contd.

S. No.	*Less Popular Motives*	*Means*
9.	To understand the benefits and the losses of deforestation	3.24
10.	To know more about the high yielding varieties of poularties	3.21
11.	To know about better methods of agriculture	3.18
12.	To know about different pesticides, fertilisers and their extent of use etc.	3.13
13.	To know about the high yielding varieties of seeds and their treatment	3.09
14.	To understand political scenario	2.96
15.	To know the uses of different fertilisers	2.93
16.	To Learn about different methods of irrigation	2.88

Unit II: Causes for Drop-out from the ATP Centre

Dropout phenomena is universal to all the educational programmes with varying degrees at various levels. This is also true in case of Total Literacy Programmes participants. It is necessary to identify the causes for drop-out from the programme and the factors influencing this phenomena. The knowledge in this area not only helps in identifying the factors affecting the drop-out phenomena but also helpful in formulating suitable strategies to prevent the drop-outs. Keeping this in view, the causes for drop-out was collected from the selected drop-outs and the information collected was pooled together and analysed.

(1) Categorisation of the Causes for Drop-outs

The causes for the drop-out expressed by the drop-out sample were categorised into three groups based on the intensity of the causes expressed by the drop-outs the causes were classified by following the criteria mean cause ± 1/2 SD. As per this criterion, the causes having mean 3.59 and more were treated as more popular causes and items falling between 3.55 and 3.12

as popular and less than 3.11 as less popular. Based on the above criterion, out of 33 items, 8 were found to be more popular, 17 popular and remaining 8 less popular causes.

The more popular, popular and less popular causes for drop out from ATP centres are presented in the following pages in three different tables.

Table 4 presents the more popular causes for drop-outs as checked by the total sample and the items were presented in descending order based on the mean value. The items considered as popular causes for drop-out along with their respective mean values are presented in Table 5. The Table 6 shows the list of causes which were found to be less popular causes for drop out.

Table 4

More Popular Causes for Drop-out from ATP Centres

S.No.	*Popular Causes*	*Mean*
1.	Admitted in the centre by force	4.08
2.	Since there is no use of education	4.01
3.	Discouraged by others	3.87
4.	Mocking by others	3.82
5.	Because of ill-health	3.76
6.	Physical tiredness due to heavy work	3.73
7.	There is no new thing to learn	3.63
8.	Inadequate facilities in the centre	3.59

From the above tables, it is clear that the causes expressed by the participants for not attending the centres are due to the lack of understanding about the importance of education in their present day-to-day life and for their future, health, tiredness after the days heavy work, physical facilities at the centre, lack of functionaries support, lack of encouragement from family members and community etc. As the above items shows that the environment building activities of the programme was not so effective and the community was not motivated properly to participate in the centres and to encourage the neighbours to send

Table 5

Popular causes for Drop-out from ATP Centres

S.No.	*Popular Causes*	*Mean*
1.	The Programme functionaries behaviour is not up to mark	3.55
2.	The centre is not functioning properly	3.46
3.	The location of the centre is far away	3.42
4.	No lighting facility for running the centre	3.41
5.	The activities of the centre is not interesting	3.38
6.	Timings of the centre is not suitable	3.37
7.	Information was not explained in an understandable manner	3.36
8.	Lack of sufficient quantity of learning materials	3.35
9.	There is no relationship between the daily life and the lessons taught in the centre	3.35
10.	To much work during the season	3.27
11.	Migration for getting the work	3.25
12.	Busy due to domestic work	3.25
13.	Resistance from the elders of the house	3.25
14	No body is available to take care of the children in the house	3.21
15.	Lack of proper encouragement from the family members	3.17
16.	Lack of interest in the education	3.17
17.	No body explained about the uses of education	3.12

their children to the centres. Hence under mopping up programme steps should be taken to create suitable and conducive environment for the promotion of literacy among the community.

Table 6

Less Popular Causes for Drop-out from ATP Centres

S.No.	*Less Popular Causes*	*Mean*
1.	Migration to other village due to marriage	3.11
2.	False promises of the officials	3.08
3.	It is enough with signature	3.07
4.	Unable to read and write in specified time along with others	3.05
5.	No need of education	3.05
6.	Wide gap in social and economic status between literacy workers and learners	3.01
7.	Inadequate knowledge of the literacy volunteer	2.92
8.	Lack of cordial relationship with co-learners	2.80

Unit III : Suitability of Learning Materials

The aim of the N.L.M. is to cover a large number of literates with-in shortest possible time through peoples participation, involvement of voluntary agencies and by strengthening the existing programme. The NLM is not only a peoples mission but also a Technology Mission. It does not mean mearly lighting, ventilation, black board, slate, duster, pencil, chalk but also improvement in the content and methodology of teaching, quickening the pace of learning by overall reduction in the duration of learning and making learning a lively, resilient and worth while experience and not a boring and monotonous exercise. As a result of this, the Improved Pace and Content of Learning (IPCL) method was adopted for preparation of teaching learning materials. In this method, the learner start learning through a meaningful sentences rather than by learning alphabetically. As a result of this new method of learning, the learners were in confusion in view of their previous knowledge of alphabetical method of learning language. However, this new method was adopted throughout the country in view of its positive aspects.

The Akshara Thapasman programme of Chittoor district is aimed to eradicate illiteracy in the age group of 9-35 years. The children in the age group of 9-14 years was also included in the target group with the belief that if the left overs, drop-outs of formal system were not taken care again they may enter into the ocean of illiteracy and become future target of adult eduction programme. In order to stop the inflow of future illiterates into this ocean, the programme planners also included this group as target under the present programme. No doubt that all precautions were taken to make the programme as success.

In spite of heterogeneity of the target group i.e. is 9-14 years and 15-35 years, the programme planners gone ahead with a single primer prepared based on IPCL method for all the groups to provide literacy and awareness. The above components are more suitable to the adults as they are more matured and actively participating in the world of work. Contrary to the above the children in the age group of 9-14 years are less matured and are not aware of worldly affairs which are not so important in their day to day life. Hence in view of the new teaching/learning methods and heterogeneity of target group an attempt was made to measure the field functionaries attitude about the suitability of the learning materials to the two groups of participants and in terms of content, presentation, style of writing, pace of learning, utility in their day to day life etc. The information collected in this regard was analysed and presented in the Table 7.

The Table 7 shows the sample size, mean, S.D. and obtained 'F' value between different groups of functionaries.

Table 7

Level of Attitude, Mean, S.Ds and 'F' Value

S.No.	*Groups*	*N*	*Mean*	*SD*	*F*
1.	Low positive attitude	70	118.11	8.17	
2.	Positive attitude	70	141.28	6.43	267.26**
3.	More positive attitude	60	167.10	10.75	

**Significant at 0.01 level.

The findings presented in the table shows that the obtained mean attitude scores of different groups of functionaries categorised according to the criterion mean attitude score ± ½ S.D. The trend of the attitudinal scores clearly reveals that more than 2/3 of the chosen sample rated the learning materials more suitable to the participants of the Total Literacy Campaign. However the obtained mean attitudinal score of the 1/3 of the chosen functionaries were also found to be low in their opinion about the suitability of the materials. Hence the trend can be taken as a positive stand of the functionaries towards the suitability of the materials to the target participating in ATP The obtained 'F' value between the three groups shows that the mean difference is significant. In other words the learning materials utilised in the ATP in Chittoor district is appropriate in all aspects to the children (age group 9-14 years) and the adults (15-35) and the IPCL method found to be accept to the target.

Hence, it is necessary to enlighten the functionaries about positive aspects of the teaching learning materials used in the programme through pre-service and in-service training programmes. So as to equip them to convenience the target of the programme to accept the same. On the whole the materials prepared and utilised based on IPCL Method were found to be acceptable to the functionaries and effective in terms of participants. In view of the above it is recommended to use the materials in NFE Programme for the new entrants.

Unit IV : Performance in Literacy

(i) Adult Learners Performance in Literacy

The achievement test developed by the investigator was administered to selected sample of the ATP centres in order to assess the extent of literacy achieved by them. Further the collected data was also analysed literacy component wise viz reading, writing arithmetic and literacy. Further the sample was also classified into three groups as low achievers, medium achievers and high achievers based on the criterion group mean achievement ± ½ S.D. The analysed data was presented in the Table 8. The Table 8 shows the sample size, mean, S.D., F values obtained by different groups of learners in reading, writing, arithmetic and literacy. The result presented in Table 8 discloses that the total mean achievement of thee learners in literacy is 46.45 which is far below the standard set by the N.L.M. for literacy norm. The achievement in other components viz. Reading,

Table 8

Mean Achievement Score, SD and Respective F Values Obtained by ATP Participants in Reading, Writing, Arithmetic and in Literacy

Sl. No.	*Component*	*Group*	*N*	*Mean*	*SD*	*F*	*Total Mean*	*SD*
1.	Reading	Low	174	9.07	2.64	243.37**	17.65	7.45
		Medium	270	17.58	2.36			
		High	156	27.35	4.34			
2.	Writing	Low	146	7.83	2.65			
		Medium	286	14.35	1.62	275.14**	14.20	6.90
		High	168	23.36	3.58			
3.	Arithmetic	Low	174	8.02	2.26			
		Medium	222	15.28	2.19	330.61**	15.47	7.68
		High	204	24.59	3.60			
4.	Literacy	Low	174	25.55	6.45			
		Medium	162	45.29	4.41	325.44**	46.45	17.06
		High	204	65.53	7.54			

** Significant at 0.01 level.

Writing and Arithmetic is 17.65, 14.20 and 15.47 respectively. The trend of the achievement in literacy and in its components clearly demonstrate that level of literacy attained by the learners is very low and superficial, if the learners were not taken proper care, again, it is likely that they may relapse into illiteracy. The classification of the learners based on their achievement scores in literacy and its components clearly shows that more than ¼ of them were almost illiterates with little skill in literacy. Hence it is necessary to equip the learners in literacy by exposing them to more visual literacy so as to make them to recognise, recollect and strengthen the skill of identification. Further more opportunities may be created to use this newly learnt skill in their day to day life.

(ii) Comparison of the ATP participants with NFE (Stage II & III) and School Children (Class III & IV) in their Achievement in Literacy

In order to understand the standard of the literacy achieved by the ATP learners, the literacy test was administered to the N.F.E. stage II & III learners and class III & IV children of formal schools not only to understand the comparative literacy possessed by them but also to identify suitable entry point for the ATP participants in the Non-Formal and Formal Sectors. The knowledge of this aspect is very essential as the target covered by the T.L.Cs is also covered by the N.F.E. group i.e. 9-14 years and these group can be counselled properly for continuation of their education by entering at multiple entry points in the above systems of education. The collected data was analysed and presented in the Table 2.

Table 9 shows the mean achievement scores in literacy obtained by the participants belonging to A.T.P., N.F.E. and school system.

The result presented in the above table discloses that the ATP participants do differ significantly with the school children and N.F.E. participants in writing and arithmetic with low level of achievement. On the other hand the achievement scores in reading and literacy does not differ significantly. However the

Table 9. Mean Achievement in Literacy, S.Ds Obtained by Participants Belonging to ATP, NFE (Stage II and III) Class III & IV, and Obtained 't' Values Between ATP and Each One of the Above Groups

S.No.	Component	ATP	NFE				School			
		Mean & SD 1	Stage II Mean & SD 2	't' 1 vs 2	Stage III Mean & SD 3	't' 1 vs 3	Class III Mean & SD 4	't' 1 vs 4	Class IV Mean & SD 5	't' 1 vs 5
1.	Reading	17.65	17.53	0.11@	18.24	0.59@	17.60	0.09@	18.84	1.13@
		(7.45)	(7.97)		(6.94)		(5.61)		(7.51)	
2.	Writing	14.20	10.74	3.60**	16.16	2.08*	17.78	3.90**	18.26	4.22**
		(6.90)	(5.97)		6.53		6.91		6.82	
3.	Arithmetic	15.47	16.78	2.00*	17.49	1.97*	16.82	1.98*	17.40	1.43@
		7.68	6.63		6.93		5.70		6.19	
4.	Literacy	46.47	45.95	0.25@	50.14	1.70@	52.25	2.84**	52.68	2.95*
		17.06	9.99		13.5		11.25		12	

@ Not Significant * Significant at 0.05 level ** significant at 0.01 level

trend of the obtained scores shows that A.T.P. participants has scored low in comparison with N.F.E. stage III and Class III and IV of Formal Schools. It clearly demonstrates that the suitable entry point for the A.T.P. participants in N.F.E sector is stage II and Class II or III of formal schools.

Unit V : Relationship Between Volunteers Attitude and their Effectiveness

Volunteer is the key person and actual doer of adult education programme at the grass root level and the success of the programme largely lies on the performance of the volunteer at the community level. The efficiency of the volunteer in performing various roles assigned to him both inside the centre and in the community is governed by the attitude possessed by him towards various aspects of the programme. It is true that functionaries with positive attitude towards their work will be more committed and fully involved in discharging their duties. The efficiency of the volunteers not only disclosed through the effective organisation of centre activities and in the promotion of literacy environment but his efficiency is also reflected in the performance of the participants in literacy. Keeping this in view, in this section an attempt was made to find out the relationship between attitude possessed by the volunteers and his efficiency in terms of his learners achievement in literacy. The data thus generated in this regard was analysed and presented in the Table 10.

Table 10

Mean Attitude Scores, SD, F and X^2 Values Obtained by the Volunteers Belongs to Different Levels of Effectiveness

Sl. No.	*Variable*	*Group*	*N*	*Mean Attitude Score*	*S.D*	*'F'*	*X^2*
1.	Effectiveness	Low	80	131.80	22.15	0.67@	2.54@
2.		Moderate	54	135.15	18.82		
3.		More	66	137.45	20.95		

@ Not Significant.

The table 10 shows the variabes, sample sizes, mean, S.Ds, x^2/F values obtained by differnt groups of volunteers.

The findings presented in the above table disclosed that the association between the two variables were found to be not significant as the calculated chi-square value is found to be lower than the table value. Further the 'F' value calculated between different groups of volunteers also found to be not significant. However the trend of the obtained mean attitude scores shows that there is a close association between efficiency and possession of positive attitude. Hence it is advised that curriculum for the pre-service and in-service training programmes, may be restructured to build up the positive attitude towards various aspects of the programme.

SECTION B

FUNCTIONING OF THE POST LITERACY CAMPAIGN

Unit I : Infrastructure Available at Janachaitanya Kendras

The Jana Chaitanya Kendras was created to ensure remediation and continuation of learning activity and to create awareness among the neo-literates with regard to Health, Environment, Family Welfare etc. It is also aimed to bring back the drop-outs to the centre and help the participants to enter into the self-learning from guided earning through functional literacy materials. It will act as a meting place for discussing the common problems of the community and to evolve suitable strategies to solve the identified problems through their own action. It also acts as a single window for providing the required information to the community by obtaining the information and materials from different sources on different activities.

In order to perform the above functions effectively all J.C.Ks should have minimum infrastructural facilities. Keeping this in view, the data relating to the infrastructural facilities available in the J.C.Ks were collected and analysed. The findings area as follows.

(i) Location of J.C.Ks

The location of the J.C.Ks discloses that J.C.Ks are located in Panchayath office (42%), Monitor residence (35%), Temple (9%),

School (7%), Learners house and other (7%). It appears that J.C.Ks were established whereever there is accommodation and of the choice learners and conveniences were not taken care of.

The further enquiry with regard to the type of housing that was provided to the J.C.Ks reveals that the J.C.Ks were located in Kacha Houses (41%), Dabbas (26%), Hut (17%) and Pakka houses (16%). Certainly the above arrangement will not be so attractive for the neo-literates.

As the J.C.Ks are expected to perform very important task of retaining the literacy, promoting and stabilising the literacy and helping the learners to choose their own path of further education. Hence the J.C.Ks must be provided with permanent housing so as to perform its activity continuously without any hindrances and the neo-literates should feel that JCKs should be a relaxing plane and information centres.

In addition to the above J.C.Ks should also perform other functions like maintaining library, organising discussion group, dissemination of functional information, conducting sports and games etc. In view of its diversified roles, further enquiry with regard to the lighting facilities, furniture, book keeping facilities, reading room facilities etc., was made and information generated was presented in the following pages.

(ii) Lighting Facilities

The findings with regard to the lighting facilities shows that 89% of the J.C.Ks were electrified and possessed adequate lighting facilities. However the 11% of the J.C.Ks were equipped with petromax lights. It appears that the T.L.C. authorities has taken steps to see that a the J.C.Ks are equipped with adequate lighting facilities.

(iii) Furniture

The enquiry with regard to the availability of furniture shows that forty one percent of J.C.Ks were having Table and Chair for Monitor and twenty one per cent of J.C.Ks were equipped with wooden planks and mats for learners. However 28 percent of J.C.Ks were possessed almarah. From the above it appears that more than one fourth of the J.C.Ks were not possessed any furniture at all. Hence top priority may be accorded for providing minimum seating facilities both for the monitor and as well as for the participants.

(iv) Book Keeping Facility

In order to promote the taste for reading, the T.L.C. authorities are providing need based, interest based learning materials to all the J.C.Ks. In addition one or two daily news papers were also supplied. In order to maintain the above books, storage facilities are required. Keeping this in view, the existing situation in the J.C.Ks were reviewed to find out the facilities available at J.C.Ks for book keeping. The enquiry revealed that only one percent of the J.C.Ks were possessed a wooden box and two percent with trunk box and rest of the 97% of the J.C.Ks hardly have any facility to store the books. Hence it is necessary to provide atleast a trunk box to all the J.C.Ks to store the books, so that the books can be maintained for a longer period.

The information relating to the physical facilities and infrastructure available for the J.C.Ks to organise its activities clearly demonstrate that not even a single J.C.K. is equipped to perform its noble task. Hence, it is suggested that all the J.C.Ks should be provided with minimum physical facilities not only to perform its activities but also to attract and retain the neo-literates for strengthening the literacy skills lest the efforts put on for the promotion of literacy will go a waste, and there is possibility of relapsing the neo-literates into illiteracy.

Unit II : Community Attitude Towards Functioning of J.C.Ks

The list of the activities of the J.C.K. shows that the J.C.K. has to perform centre based programmes as well as community based programmes. The target of the centre based programmes are illiterates, neo-literates and literates on the other hand for community based activities such as organisation of discussion group, reading room, cultural activities, sports, games, recreational programmes, short term training programme etc., forms the entire community as target. In other wards the impact of the J.C.K. activities will be felt by not only by the participants of the programme but also the community. The functioning of the J.C.K. and its effect is also known by the community and community will also be watching the activities of the J.C.K. very keenly. Keeping this in view the attitude scale constructed for measuring the community attitude towards the functioning of J.C.K. was administered to the community. The data thus collected was analysed and presented in the Table 11. The table shows the mean community attitude scores, S.Ds, and obtained 'F' values.

Table 11

Mean Community Attitude Score, SD and 'F' Value Obtained Between Different Groups of Community

Sl. No.	*Level of attitude*	*N*	*Mean*	*S.D.*	*F*
1.	Low	66	3.31	1.32	
2.	Moderate	78	3.47	1.12	0.97@
3.	More	56	3.76	1.18	

@ Not significant.

The results presented in the above table clearly demonstrates that one third of the community representatives were possessing low positive attitude towards the J.C.K. activities. Contrary to the above 28 percent of the community representatives have convenienced that the J.C.Ks were serving the community effectively. In addition to the above, 39 per cent of the community representatives are of the moderate in their opinion towards the activities of the J.C.K. On the whole majority of the chosen community representatives were of the opinion that the J.C.Ks were functioning effectively in the community. It is a well-coming trend and its efficiency may be further enhanced so that all the community should feel proud of its existence in their community.

Unit III : Community Support for J.C.K. Activities

The Jana Chaitanya Kendras were established for promoting the self-help activities among the community for their betterment. In other words J.C.Ks not only provides inputs but also draws some of the aspects of the community as its input for effective organisation of its activities. Keeping this in view the community support scale was administered to the selected sample of community to understand the extent of support provided by the community to the J.C.K. activities. The knowledge of this helps to understand the reputation enjoyed by the J.C.K. in the community. The data generated in this aspect was analysed and presented in the Table 12.

Table 12

Mean Support Scores, SD and 'F' Value Obtained by the Different Community Groups

Sl. No.	*Groups*	*N*	*Mean support*	*S.D.*	*F*
1.	More	42	3.59	1.09	
2.	Moderate	62.	3.53	1.25	0.11@
3.	Less	96	3.46	1.28	

@ Not significant.

The trend of the mean support scores presented in the table discloses that 21% of the J.C.Ks enjoyed more support from the community, followed by 31% moderate support and nearly half of the J.C.Ns have obtained less support from the community. Further the trend clearly demonstrate that the community is using the J.C.Ks for its advantage but not reciprocating their support for its activities. Hence it is necessary to create awareness among the community that the J.C.Ks are not external agencies but created by the community, for the community, of the community and they should actively participate and manage the activities of the J.C.K. A special training may be organised for the monitors in ways and means of obtaining the support from the community.

Unit IV : Attitude of the Neo-Literates Towards the Functioning of J.C.Ks in Retention of Literacy

The Jana Chaitanya Kendras were created for the benefit of the neo-literates not only to strengthen the newly learnt skill of literacy but also to help them to acquire the suitable skills by them and to demand and to obtain their rightful share in the development activities. In other words the successful performance of J.C.Ks largely lies in the participation and utilisation of the neo-literates in the J.C.K. activities and facilities respectively. The effective participation of new-literates in the J.C.K. activities and utilisation of the opportunities created by the J.C.K. depends on largely governed the attitude possessed by the neo-literates towards the various activities of the J.S.N. Keeping this in view an attempt was made to identify the type of attitude possessed by the neo-literates towards the various activities of the J.C.K. in retention of literacy among them by administering an attitude scale developed by the investigator to the selected neo-literates. The data thus generated was pooled together analysed and presented in the Table 13.

Table 13

Mean Attitude Scores, SD and 'F' Value Obtained Between Different Groups of Neo-literates

Sl. No.	*Groups*	*N*	*Mean*	*S.D.*	*F*
1.	Low attitude	70	3.30	1.19	
2.	Medium attitude	68	3.35	1.10	0.54@
3.	More attitude	62	3.63	1.28	

@ Not significant.

The results presented in the above table clearly demonstrate that 31% of the selected sample of neo-literates possessed more positive attitude towards the various activities of the J.C.K. In addition to the above 34% of the neo-literates were of the opinion that the activities are satisfactory. However 35% of the neo-literates possessed low opinion towards the activities of the J.C.K. Hence it is necessary to change the attitude of the neo-literates by organising the activities of the J.C.K. in a more attractive and efficient manner suitable to the neo-literates.

Unit V : Problems Faced By the Monitors in Organising J.C.K. Activities

In order to conduct various activities of the J.C.Ks, each J.C.K. is manned by two monitors. The monitors are volunteers working on a non-remunerative basis. The monitor in-charge of

Post-literacy and Continuing education should promote the literacy among the neo-literates motivate the adults to attend the J.C.Ks, to distribute the books for neo-literates, Organises short term training programmes, Churcha Mandals, village parliaments etc.

The list of the functions unravels that the monitor is in-charge for diversified roles and organising all the activities of the J.C.K. is not easy to achieve it. In view of the multidimensional activities of the J.C.Ks, the monitor should interact with heterogeneous groups in the society. In this process the monitor has to face innumerable problems both personal and professional and has to overcome this with tact. In order to make his job easy

Table 14

Prominent Problems

Sl. No.	*Problems Items*	*Mean*
1.	Lack of provision for honorarium to the monitors	3.98
2.	Lack of suitable cooperation from development department officials for implementation of the decisions of the churcha mandals	3.93
3.	Lack of suitable sports and games materials at the JCK	3.92
4.	Borrowing of good numbers of books by the educated, leaving little scope for neo-liteates	3.84
5.	Lack of audiovisual aids to disseminate the information to the learners in JCK	3.82
6.	Lack of recognition for monitors on par with social workers	3.81
7.	JCK's inability to provide training in suitable occupational skills to women due to lack of cooperation from development departments	3.73
8.	Lack of provision for the production of posters and charts for the propagation of JCK activities	3.66
9.	Lack of suitable post-literacy materials for the promotion of literacy	3.61
10.	Lack of information in development programme	3.58
11.	Lack of effective cooperation from the village leaders for implementation of the decisions of the churcha mandals	3.50
12.	Irrelevancy of the available books in JCK to the interests of adults	3.49

Table 15
Moderate Problems

Sl. No.	*Problems Items*	*Mean*
1.	Getting return of the books from borrowers	3.47
2.	Lack of training and suitable materials for monitors to conduct cultural programmes	3.43
3.	Lack of suitable infrastructure for the organisation of sports and games	3.34
4.	Irregular supply of newspapers to JCK	3.33
5.	Lack of suitable facilities to motivate the community to participate in the Churcha Mandals	3.32
6.	Lack of adequate facilities for the organisation of activities in all affiliated hamlets of the JCK	3.26
7.	Lack of adequate lighting facilities in JCK	3.23
8.	Inability to provide different occupational skills to neo-literates	3.22
9.	Traditional beliefs and customs becoming obstacles in organising activities relating to women's empowerment	3.21
10.	Inadequate training for monitors for the effective implementation of JCK activities in cooperation with local experts	3.16
11.	Ability to maintain harmonious relationship with villagers	3.13
12.	Lack of equal participation on the part of men and women	3.13
13.	Lack of cooperation from the school system for reinduction of dropout children	3.12

the knowledge of the anticipated problems of monitor will be a boon for the programme implementors. The identification the problems not only helps the monitor to know the anticipated problems but also to tackle them easily. It also helps to equip the perspective monitors and working monitor through pre-service training and In service training. Keeping this in view the problem scale was administered to selected monitors. The data thus generated was analysed and the problems were categorised into three groups based on problem mean score ± 1/2 S.D. as prominent problems, moderate problems and less prominent problems. The division shows that 12 items were found to be prominent, 13 moderate and 13 as less prominent problems. The prominent and moderate problems are Tables 14 and 15.

From the above tables it appears that most of the prominent problems were related to materials, cooperation from villagers and officials, vocational skills programmes, and about monitor status and honorarium. The moderate problems identified covers the items like inadequate infrastructure, training, participation, cooperation from different sources for effective functioning of J.C.Ks.

In view of the above problems, it is advised that all J.C.Ks should be equipped with necessary reading materials, audiovisual aids, and developmental information. The monitor efficiency should be enhanced by exposing them to the constant training. Further steps may be taken to gear-up the enthusiasm generated among the community earlier, so as to make the community to aware of the utility of the education in their day-to-day life and help them to demand their share in the development programmes initiated by the Government.

Unit VI : Performance of the J.C.Ks

As mentioned earlier the J.C.K. has to perform a number of roles with in the centre and as well as in the community. In order to measure the performance of the J.C.K. its performance in all its roles should be considered. In order to arrive at, suitable numerical values were assigned to measure its extent of performance in all the identified functions. The mean values of J.C.K. performance was arrived by adding the values assigned to the different roles. The J.C.Ks were categorised based on the criterion mean performance score ± 1/2 S.D. into there categories viz. Poor, Moderate and good. The results were presented in the following Table 16.

Table 16

Mean Performance Values Obtained by Different Groups of JCKs

S.No.	*Level of performance*	*N*	*Mean*
1.	Poor	54	<131.23
2.	Moderate	72	131.24 to 139.23
3.	Good	74	194.24>

The results presented in the above table unvels that more than 2/3 of the J.C.Ks were found to be effectively discharging their functions. On the other hand more than 1/4 of the J.C.Ks performance is very poor and requires to take up immediate steps to improve its performance by identifying the weak points and strengthening them.

Unit VII : Performance of the Monitors

In order to institutionalise the Post-literacy programmes in the Total Literacy Campaign of Chittoor District, a new institution called Jana Chaitanya Kendram was established. It is distinct from J.S.N. of earlier Adult Education Programmes. The shift in focus from mear teaching and learning to a life long continuous "learning for Life" was evident in its nomenclature. The efforts in post-literacy therefore is to channelise the new discovered latent energies towards national building. As result, it encompassed within its ambit all that is needed to conscientious people.

The components of the activity schedule of J.C.Ks were daily newspaper, weakly broad sheet, weekly discussion forum, village parliament visits to Government offices, teaching the post-literacy test and writing news on literacy walls. The J.C.Ks are aimed to be the hub of all developmental activities under the post-literacy strategy that would go on for years. In view of its role each J.C.K. is manned by a monitor who is expected to perform all the above tasks. In other words the monitor has to perform various roles inside and out side the J.C.K. The monitor effectiveness can be seen in successful performance of the roles assigned to him. Keeping the above in view the unit is aimed to identify the performance and grouping the effective groups of monitors based on the mean performance ± 1/2 SD criterion. The monitor effectiveness scale is designed by the investigator was administered to the selected sample for obtaining the relevant data. The data thus collected analysed as mentioned above and presented in the following Table 17.

Table 17

Groups of Monitors according to their Effectiveness

S.No.	*Level of effectiveness*	*Percentage*
1.	More effective	34%
2.	Effective	39%
3.	Less effective	27%

From the above table it appears that 1/3 of the monitors selected for the study were found to be very effective in their performance. Further 39 percent of the sample were also found to be effective, contrary to the above 27 percent of the monitors were found to be less effective. In other words more than 1/4 of the Monitors were not able to perform their functions at the satisfactory level. Hence steps may be taken to equip the less effective monitors by organising in-service training programme by identifying the weak points of the monitors.

Unit VIII : Field Functionaries Attitude Towards Training, Monitoring and Evaluation

The success of the Total Literacy Campaign not only lies in effective teaching of literacy at the grassroots level but also the training provided to the field functionaries, monitoring and evaluation of the programme to identify the deficiencies and short comings of the programme and to overcome them by

Table 18

Mean Attitude Scores, S.D. and 'F' Values Obtained by Different Groups of Field Functionaries on Training, Monitoring and Evaluation

S.No.	*Variable*	*Group*	*N*	*Mean*	*S.D*	*F Value*
1.	Training	Low	84	133.30	26.30	
		Moderate	38	135.31	26.49	1.38 @
		More	78	142.64	25.08	
2.	Monitoring & Evaluation	Low	70	133.14	34.04	
		Moderate	76	138.81	18.73	0.73 @
		More	54	140.66	22.69	

equipping the functionaries through training at the initial stage itself. No doubt that the T.L.C. has its own mechanism of Training. Monitoring and Evaluation. The end users of this three components are field functionaries and the efficiency of this three components are felt by the functionaries. Hence the efficiency of this three components can be identified by measuring the attitudes of the field functionaries towards them. Hence in order to measure the efficiency of the components the scale was administered to field functionaries. The obtained data was analysed was presented in the Table 18.

The results presented in the above table clearly demonstrate that the functionaries classified into different groups based on the criterion mean ± 1/2 S.D. does not differ significantly with each other in their attitude towards Training, Monitoring and Evaluation aspects of the programme. However the trend of the obtained attitude scores shows that more than half of the selected sample of the study were of the opinion that the Training, Monitoring and Evaluation were effective. On the other side more than 1/3 of selected sample were of the opinion that the above components are very weak. It shows that something is wrong with the above aspects of the programme. Hence it is suggested that the programme administration should take immediate steps to strengthen the above components to improve the quality of the programme.

Unit IX : Strength and Deficiencies of the Programme

In order to identify the strength weakness, and functionaries suggestions for the improvement of the programme, the investigator has conducted an unstructured interview with the selected sample of the study and elucidated the positive and negative aspects of the programme. The information thus collected was recorded and pool together. The pooled information on the strength weakness, and suggestions for the improvement of the programme are as follows.

(i) Strengths of the Programme

(a) The Environment building activity of the programme is not only successful in creating awareness about the programme among the community but also enlightened the community

about the importance of education in their day-to-day life and for their future.

(b) The programme created awareness among the community about various development programmes initiated by the government and their right to utilise them for their own-development. The community is well aware of the programmes and able to demand their share.

(c) The people are aware that the govt. has created official machinery as intermediate agency between community and the government. As a result of the programme the community is more aware of their strengths and is free in their interaction with govt. officials and development agencies.

(d) The children (9-14 years) participating in the programme is also aware of various educational opportunities available for them to shape their destiny.

(e) The educated and youth are well conscious about their roles and responsibilities towards the development of the fellow beings in particular and the community as a whole.

(f) There was a dramatic improvement in the parents awareness about their responsibility towards their children education and as a result the enrolment in the schools has gone-up and dropout rate at the schools has gone down.

(g) The programme has created a sort of we-feeling among the community. The community is in a position to understand its own problems and has ability to sort out them at their own level.

(ii) The Weaknesses of the Programme

No doubt the programme was chalked-out systematically to make it a grand success by promoting literacy in the age group of 9-35 years', but in-course of implementation of the programme with an intention to solve them with the assistance of appropriate authority. The weakness of the programme as spelt-out by the functionaries are as follows.

(a) In order to gear-up the programme, administrators has involved the school teachers at all stages and capacities. As a result of too-much involvement of the teachers, the community is of the opinion that the teachers were not is position to concentrate on their prime responsibility of school teaching.

(b) The awareness generated by the programme has tremendous effect not only on their lives but also on the community. As a result of this all sections of the people were started demanding their due share in the community. As a natural effect the affluent sections of the community started intervening in the programme to sabotage it by preventing the people to taste the fruits of the programme.

(c) One of the major drawbacks of the programme identified by the functionaries is the wide gap between the completion of the literacy programme and initiation of the follow-up programme. As a result of this the enthusiasm generated in the initial stages has evaporated and again requires a fresh breeze to push the programme into the regular track so as to move it smoothly.

(d) The aim of the programme is not only to promote literacy but also help the participants to earn extra bugs by learning and using the new skill. However in practice the programme is not able to move beyond the literacy stage. Hence there is a need to integrate the literacy with some sort of vocational skill suitable to their lives so as to help them to use it in their day to day life.

(e) The success of the NLM largely revolves around its basic component Viz. Area specific, Time bound, and voluntarism. No doubt the voluntarism, generated a new wave of enthusiasm among all sections of the people to contribute their might. The volunteer at the gross-root level is the key person responsible for taking the programme into the hearts of the people. As on date neither they were recognised nor appreciated for their hard work. Hence it is a high time to recognise the services of the volunteer and make them to feel proud of their services to the human kind.

(*f*) Though the programme is in operation for the lost three years, all the functionaries were drawn from various other departments and moulded them suitable to this programme. This was done keeping in view of the temporary nature of the programme. Now all the functionaries are well aware that they should go back to their original work, after completing the present assignment. As a result, cracks are started to appear in the programme administration. Hence the functionaries are of the opinion that there is a need to have a team of full-time committed functionaries for the programme not only to fill the newly arised cracks but also to take the programme into the future.

(*g*) The training imparted to the field functionaries at all levels is not sufficient for catering to their needs, duties and found to be week. Hence it should be strengthened.

(*h*) Though priority was accorded for the coverage of women, but the rate of participation of women (illiterates as well the functionary level) is very low.

(iii) Suggestions for Improvement of the Programme

The field functionaries interviewed were of the opinion that the programme can be made successful by taking the necessary action on the following.

1. In order to retain the tempo generated in the initial period of launching the programme, the Jathas, Cultural Programmes, Processions, meetings between functionaries and community sector levels, mass media propaganda about the TLC may be organised at regular intervals.

2. The Training Curriculum for the functionaries at various levels may be restructured based on the functionaries needs and the required skills and abilities may be developed through pre-service and in-service trainings.

3. In addition to the primers, supplementary, materials may be provided to the Instructors/monitors covering various current and relevant aspects.

4. The regular monitoring may be made with regard to the participation of the target and suitable steps may be taken to ensure the regular attendance of the target in the adult education centres.
5. The dropouts should be motivated to return to the adult education centres by helping them to realise the importance of literacy and education in their day-to-day life.
6. The school system may be strengthened to cover all the eligible children and to reduce to maximum extent of absenteeism and dropout phenomenon.
7. Special care should be taken for the slow learners and should be helped to learn on par with others.
8. All educated and unemployed youth should be involved in the programme not as volunteers but as committed citizens.
9. The functionaries at various levels of the programme should be recruited or drawn not only based on their qualification but based on their aptitude towards the literacy work.
10. The drafting of formal school teachers to the adult education programmes should be stopped immediately as involvement of this group not only disturbing the functions of the normal school work but also the teachers are carrying their old faiths, traditions and practices along with them and these are coming in their way of functioning.
11. The supervision of the area coordinates/resource persons is not frequent and effective. Hence supervision should be made compulsory and grass root level functionaries should be guided and counselled properly.
12. No doubt that evaluation process is in built and this should not be limited to literacy along but it should be able to measure the impact of literacy on the individual and as well as society as a whole.

13. The gap between the closure of the literacy phase and starting of post literacy phase should be reduced or it should start immediately.
14. The post-literacy materials should be not only based on the needs and interest of the neo-literates but also the standard of literacy possessed by them.
15. Along with post-literacy and continuing education provision may be made to develop suitable vocational skills.
16. The Janachaitanya Kendra should act as a information window for the neo-literates.
17. All the developmental assistance ment for the community should be processed through the JCKs.
18. All the developmental departments should use the JCKs for propagation and implementation of their programme.

6

Summary and Conclusion

Introduction

Recognising that the adult education would be a means for reducing economic, social and gender disparities, the Government of India has launched more than 420 District Total Literacy Campaigns through out the country under National Literacy Mission to cover more than 100 million illiterates by 2005 years. The Chittoor district is one of the first districts in Andhra Pradesh to launch the total literacy campaign as Akshara Thapasman Programme to cover 6.25 lakh illiterates in the are group of 9- 35 years. Now the comparison has entered into third phase by launching moping-up of programme to cover the new entrants, dropouts and uncovered segments of the target. The progress of the programme was evaluated both by externally as well as internal evaluation teams. The findings of the above clearly demonstrated that during the first phase 3.25 lakh illiterates where made literates and in the second phase along with the post-literacy stage again 2 lakh illiterates were covered. In order to cover the rest of the target, efforts are being made through moping-up of the programme and by launching village continuing education centres through the districts. In view of the current efforts, the present study was formulated to strengthen the hands of the programme administrators with the information which is not available so as to make use of this in their efforts to eradicate the illiteracy.

Review of Literature

Keeping in view of the above, all the literature available was reviewed to identify the extent of information generated and gaps that are existing. The available review of the literature was classified as review on Literacy phase and Post-literacy phase. The studies on Literacy phase [Krishnamurthy (1993), Karve Institute of Social Services (1994), Centre for Media Studies (1994), Mustaq Ahmad (1994), TISS (1993), 1993a, 1993b), Santha Mohan (1994), Paul and Sarvanan (1993), Kishore Attavar (1994), Anil Bhatt (1993), Sardar Patel, Institute of Economic and Social Research (1993, 1993 a, 1994, 1994 a), Om Mehta (1994), Gokulo Parkeh (1994), The Institute of Social Science (1993), Indradev (1993), Desh Pande (1993), Tribal and Harijan Research-Cum-Training Institute (1993), Gopal Krishna Reddy (1993), Shastry and Chariyuu (1993), Council for Social Development (1993), Michale Tharakan (1990), Denzil Saldhanha (1992 and 1992a)]. Mustaq Ahamad and others (1992) and Sidda Gowda (1996) evaluated the different total literacy campaign districts on a single aspect i.e. achievement in literacy. Hence the information generated relates to the extent of literacy achieved by the participants in a given time frame. But no efforts were made to identify the motives of the participants, causes for the dropouts, participants and volunteers attitude towards the materials used etc.

The review on post literacy phase shows that Vasumathi (1992), Nair and others (1992), Muthuchamy (1992), Adhilakshmi (1993), Reddeppa (1993), Padmanabhaiah and Kumarswamy (1995), SRC of Karnataka (1995), DAE (1994), Janardhana Rao V (1996), Mohanty and Prusty (1996) and P.A. Reddy (1996) have conducted studies to identify various aspects of post-literacy programmes in isolation and no attempt was made to evaluate the post-literacy programme comprehensively covering all aspects so as to have a clear picture of the functioning of the post-aspects of the programme, present study was formulated to cover all phases i.e. literacy and post-literacy of the total literacy campaign to identify the factors contributing for its success.

Statement of the Problem

A study of the certain aspects of the Akshara Thapasman Programme (Total Literacy Campaign) of Chittoor district, A.P.

Scope of the Study

The scope of the present study is very wide as the aspects planned to cover are varied and numerous. However broadly speaking, the present investigation intended to identify the motives of the participants for attending the ATP centres, causes for the dropouts, functionaries opinion towards the suitability of the learning materials, extent of literacy achieved by the learners, volunteers attitude and their effectiveness. In addition to the above, study also intended to cover the aspects relating to the post literacy programme viz., availability of infrastructure for JCKs community attitude and support to the JCKs, monitors problems, neo-literates and field functionaries attitude towards JCKs and finally the performance of JCKs.

Need of the Study

The aim of the National Literacy Mission is to accelerate the socio-economic development of the country by qualifying vast masses of the human resources through the promotion of literacy social consciousness and functionality among them. In order to realise the above, NLM sponsored the total literacy campaigns in the selected districts. The Chittoor district of A.P. is one among the first phase districts to implement TLC in the name of Akashra Thapasman programme (ATP). Now the programme has entered into the third phase completing the literacy and post-literacy stages. However inspite of its success in literacy and post-literacy fronts, still it is consolidating its gains and rectify-ing the deficiencies. As a result of this, there is moping-up of the programme for the new-entrants, left overs and dropouts through 100 days literacy programme. The continuing education centres are being established for the higher order learners. In view of its operation in three stages, there is a need to identify why the participants joined the programme and also left. Is it the distributed material is not attractive? The volunteers are not trained or indifferent?

The post-literacy centres are managed by monitors. The role of monitor is divergent and is responsible not only for promotion of literacy but also to make it consolidated. In this process, monitor has to encounter a number of problems. The effectiveness of the Jana Chaitanya Kendras are largely depends on the performance of the monitors and the community support received by them. As the field functionaries are drawn from various walks of life, they should be thoroughly trained not only to equip them required skills and knowledge but also to act as a change agents. In order to facilitate the functionaries working and adults participating in the JCKs requires certain infrastructural of facilities. Hence it is also necessary to identify the infrastructural facilities at the JCKs. The programme will be successful only if all the aspects system performs well or otherwise the investment made in terms of man-hours, money, material will go a wast. Hence, keeping in view of the above, the present study was formulated with the following objectives.

Objectives of the Study

1. To assess the standard of education received by the participants in Akshara Thapasman Programme.
2. To suggest appropriate entry point into the system of formal education and non-formal education programme to the participants of the Akshara Thapasman Programme.
3. To find out the motives of the participants for attending the Akshara Thapasman Programme.
4. To find out the reasons for dropping out from the Akshara Thapasman Centres.
5. To study the suitability of learning materials used in the Akshara Thapasman Centres.
6. To study the relationship between volunteers attitude towards Akshara Thapasman Programme and their effectiveness in terms of the participants' achievement in literacy and awareness.
7. To find out the availability of the infrastructure for the organisation of Jana Chaitanya Kendras.

8. To assess the community opinion towards the functioning of Jana Chaitanya Kendras.
9. To assess the community support received by the monitors for effective organisation of Jana Chaityanya Kendras.
10. To find out the neo-literates' opinion about the functioning of Jana Chaitanya Kendras.
11. To identify the difficulties of monitors in implementing the objectives of Jana Chaitanya Kendras.
12. To suggest probable solutions to the difficulties for effective functioning of Jana Chaitanya Kendras.
13. To assess the performance of monitors of JCKs.
14. To ascertain the opinion of the field functionaries viz., Mandal Coordinators, Village Coordinators, Volunteers, JCK monitors with regard to
    - Training
    - Monitoring
    - Evaluation
    - Strengths of the programme
    - Weaknesses of the programme and
    - Suggestions for improving the quality of the programme.

Methodology

(i) Construction of Tools

In order to generate the information on various aspects mentioned under the title objectives requires different tools. As the review of the available tools on the above aspects shows that suitable tools are not available to use them in the present study. Hence the investigator was developed the required tools. While developing tools, the following procedure was followed.

All the possible items to be incorporated in the tools were generated from different sources through personal interviews with the programme functionaries and participants. The list of the items thus generated was supplemented with the review of the relevant literature. Again this list was presented to a panel of five experts in the field for their comments and suggestions. The suggestions of the experts were carried out. The preliminary tools thus prepared consisted of two Sections. Section I intended to collect the information relating to the personal characteristics of the sample and Section. II deals with the variables intended to be measured. Appropriate scoring procedure was adopted based on the variable to be measured.

A pilot study of all the tools were conducted on a group of 100 subjects selected randomly from the appropriate groups to see the suitability of the tools used in the study. Items were selected for the final form, based on the discriminative power of the items as suggested by Edward (1969).

The final form of the tools used in the investigation are as follows.

(ii) List of the Tools

- A scale to identify the learners motives for attending Akshara Thapasman Centres.
- A scale to identify the reasons for drop-out from Akshara Thapasman Centres.
- A scale to measure the suitability of learning materials.
- A scale to measure volunteers attitude towards Akshara Thapasman programme.
- An achievement test to measure 3 R's and awareness.
- A questionaire to measure the performance of JCK.
- A scale to measure Community attitude towards JCK.
- A scale to measure Community Support towards JCK.
- A rating scale to identify the problems of the monitors.
- A scale to measure neo-literate attitudes towards JCK.
- A scale to measure monitor effectiveness.
- A scale to measure the field functionaries attitude towards effectiveness of training, monitoring and evaluation.

The Study Area and Sample

As the study is aimed to evaluate the Chittoor district of Total Literacy Campaign, the area of Chittoor district forms the study area. For the purpose of the present study, both the participants and functionaries are required as sample. The procedure adopted for the selection of the sample are as follows.

The Chittoor district consists of 66 revenue mandals. Out of the list of 66 mandals 11 mandals were selected by choosing every 6th mandal in the first stage of sample selection. There are 300 villages in these 11 mandals. In the second stage, out of 30 villages a sample of 60 villages was selected randomly by choosing not less than 5 villages from each mandal for getting various types of samples. Out of 60 villages selected, 600 ATP participants, 20 volunteers, 200 NFE teachers, were selected randomly as sample. In addition 200 and functionaries from among 3300 functionaries working at various levels in the district was also selected randomly. Apart from the above, 200 neo-literates 200 community representatives, 200 JCK monitors were also selected randomly from the 60 villages for collecting the relevant data from them. In brief, the various categories of the sample involved in the study area as follows.

1.	Akshara Thapasman participants	600
2.	Akshara Thapasman dropouts	200
3.	Akshara Thapasman volunteers	200
4.	Non-formal education instructors	200
5.	Akshara Thapasman functionaries	200
6.	Neo-literates	200
7.	Community representatives	200
8.	JCK monitories	200

Data Collection and Analysis

The tools thus developed was administered to the selected sample separately and the data was pooled and analysed by using appropriate statistical techniques.

Findings of the Study

1. The achievement scores of the TLC participants reveal that the standard of the literacy achieved by them are far below the standard of Literacy suggested by NLM.

2. The comparative achievement scores of the TLC participants, NFE stage I & II children and the children studying class III & IV shows that the TLC participants can be admitted into the stage II of NFE programme or class III of formal education as their achievement in literacy is very low.

3. The popular motives of the TLC participants are as follows.

   - To Read news paper.
   - To know more about the social evils.
   - To know how men and women are equal in all aspects.
   - To know government subsidies and loan facilities.
   - To understand the rights and duties of a citizen in democracy.
   - To maintain domestic accounts.
   - To know the prices of the essential goods.
   - To Learn to read and write.
   - To understand the content of the nutritious and balanced diet.
   - To Learn to read letters.
   - To learn to sign.
   - To know the ways and means of improving family economic status.
   - To learn to calculate daily wages.
   - To learn new and good habits from others.
   - To know the methods of preservation of food.
   - To know the better utility of voting rights.

4. The major causes for dropout of the ATP centres as expressed by the dropouts are as follows.
   - Admitting into the centre by force.
   - Since there is no use of education.
   - Discouraged by others.
   - Mocking by others.
   - Ill-health.
   - Physical tiredness.
   - There is no new thing to learn.
   - Inadepuate facilites in the centre.
5. The opinion of the functionaries reveal that the learning materials utilised in Akshara Thapasman Programme are more relevant to the children in the age group of 9-14 years.
6. The findings of the study also revealed that volunteers attitude is not significantly associated with there effectiveness however, the trend reveals that the positive attitude is associated with more efficiency.
7. The probe into the infrastructural facilities available at JCKs revealed that majority of the JCKs were located in local Panchayat offices and Monitor's house, 89% of them were equipped with proper lighting i.e. electrified, forty one percent of them were having table and chair for monitor, twenty one percent with wooden planks and mats for learners and only 28 percent possess, almara for keeping the records. It clearly demonstrate that more than half of the JCKs does not possess even physical facilities to provide comforts to the participants.
8. The community attitude towards the functioning of the JCK's revealed that 28 percent of the community were of the opinion that the JCS's were functioning effectively, 39 percent moderate and one third of them were not satisfied with regard to their performance.

9. Community support point of view 21 percent of the JCK's enjoyed the effective support, 31% received moderate support and nearly half of the JCKs (48%)) has not received any support from the communities.

10. The functioning of the JCK's in the eyes of the neo-literates revealed that one third of the neo-literate felt that it is not serving what it should have been, thirty nine percent viewed it that it is serving moderately opinion and 31 percent felt that it is functioning effectively.

11. The major problems of the monitors identified by the study were as follows.

    - Lack of provision for honorarium to the monitors.
    - Lack of suitable cooperation from development department officials for implementation of the decisions of the churcha mandals.
    - Lack of suitable sports and games materials at the JCK.
    - Borrowing of good numbers of books by the educated, leaving little scope for neo-literates.
    - Lack of audio-visual aids to disseminate the information to the learners in JCK.
    - Lack of recognition for monitors on par with social workers.
    - JCK's inability to provide training in suitable occupational skills to women due to lack of cooperation from development departments.
    - Lack of provision for the production of posters and charts for the propagation of JCK activities.
    - Lack of suitable post-literacy materials for the promotion of literacy.
    - Lack of information in developmental programs.
    - Lack of effective cooperation from the village leaders for implementation of the decisions of the churcha mandals.

- Irrelevancy of the available books in JCK to the interests of adults.

12. The overall performance of the JCK's shows that an equal number of JCK's performed effectively (37%) and (36%) moderately. On the other hand the performance of 27% JCKs were found to be very poor.
13. The performance of the monitors revealed that 27% of the monitors were found to be less effective, 39% and 34 percent found to be more effective.
14. The attitude of the field functionaries towards Training shows that 39 percent felt that the training is more effective 29% effective and 42% felt that it is not very useful.
15. The monitoring and evaluation of the programme were found to be effective (27%), moderate (38%) and less effective (35%) as per the functionaries of the programme.
16. The strengths of the programme as per the functionaries are as follows.
    - Community is fully aware about the on going adult education programme.
    - The interaction between official and community is more.
    - The community is able to utilise the development departments programmes in a more effective manner.
    - The educated are more aware about their role towards the community.
    - Increase in school enrolments.
    - The community is able to solve their problems locally.
    - Women are more conscious about their role in the development of the society.
17. Some of the weakness of the programme identified as follows.

- School teachers involvement in Literacy Programme.
- The attitude of the affluent sections of the community towards the programme.
- Lack of follow-up for the retaining the initial enthusiasm generated among the participants.
- Lack of provision for the development of vocational skills.
- Lack of recognition for the field functionaries.
- Lack of full time, regular functionaries for the programme.
- Training of the functionaries were found to be week.
- Participation of women in the programme is low.

18. Suggestions for the imporvement of the program.

- Awareness programmes about the literacy utility may be organised periodically.
- Training curriculum should be restructured.
- Supplementary resource materials should be provided to the field functionaries.
- Monitoring should be done regularly.
- Dropouts should be re-enrolled.
- School systems should be strengthened to cover all eligible children.
- All educated youth should be motivated to involve in the programme.
- Only people processing aptitude for literacy work should be recruited as functionaries.
- School teachers should not be involved in literacy programmes.
- The programme staff supervise the adult education centres regularly.

- The scope of evaluation of the learners should be widened.
- Post literacy programme should be the continuation of the literacy programme without time gap.
- Along with literacy vocational skills should be imparted.
- JCK's should be strengthened as information windows.
- JCK's should act as a nodal agency for the developmental assistance.

Bibliography

Adams (1964), *Measurement and Evaluation in Eduaction, Psychology and Guidance*, New York: Holt Rinchart and Winston Inc.

Adilakshmi (1993), *An Investigation into the Working Conditions of the Jana Shikshana Nilayams and Opinion Towards Jana Shikshana Nilayams*, Master Dissertation, S.P. Mahila University.

Anil Bhatt (1993), *Evaluation of Literacy Campaign, Tumkur District*, Ahmedabad: Indian Institute of Management.

Centre for Media Studies (1994), *Evaluation of Literacy Campaign Panipat*, New Delhi: Centre for Media Studies.

Council for Social Development (1993), *Evaluation of Literacy Campaign Karim Nagar District*, Hyderabad: CSD.

Denzil Saldanha (1992), *The Total Literacy Campaign in Sindhu Drug District: A Report of the Evaluation*, Bombay: TISS.

Denzil Saldanha (1992), *Evaluation of Total Literacy Campaign of Wardha District*, Bombay: TISS.

Deshpande (1993), *Evaluation of Literacy Campaign*, Jalna, Pune: State Resource Centre.

Directorate of Adult Education (1988), *National Literacy Mission*, New Delhi: Govt. of India.

Directorate of Adult Education (1988), *Jana Shikshan Nilayam*, New Delhi: Govt. of India.

Directorate of Adult Education (1994), *A Report of the Functioning of Jana Shikshan Nilayams 1993-94*, New Delhi: Govt. of India.

Edward AL (1994), *Statistical Analysis*, New York: Holt, Rinchart and Winston Inc.

Gokul O. Parekh (1994), *Evaluation of the Literacy Campaign of Vadodara District*, Ahmedabad: Sardar Patel Institute of Economic and Social Change.

Gopala Krishna Reddy and others (1993), *Evaluation of Literacy Campaign Vishakha Patnam District*, Vishakhapatnam: Andhra University.

Govt. of India (1995), *Evaluation of Literacy Campaign, Summary report Vol. I*, New Delhi: Ministry of Human Resource Development.

Govt. of India (1988), *National Literacy Mission*, New Delhi, Ministry of Human Resource Development.

Govt. of India (1986), *National Policy on Education*, New Delhi: Ministry of Human Resource Development.

Govt. of India (1995), *Evaluation of Literacy Campaigns, Summary*, Vol. II, New Delhi: Ministry of Human Resource Development.

Indradeva (1993), *Evaluation of Literacy Campaign*, Raipur, Ravi Shankar University.

Institute of Social Science (1993), *Evaluation of Literacy Campaign*, Goa, Bangalore: Institute of Social Sciences.

Janardhana Rao (1996), *An Enquiry into the Problems Faced by the Monitors in Jana Chaitanya Kendras*, M.Phil. Thesis, S.V. University.

Karve Institute of Social Sciences (1994), *Evaluation of the Literacy Campaign, Parbhani District*, Pune: KISS.

Kishore Attavar (1994), *Evaluation of Literacy Campaign, Shimoga District*, Bangalore: School of Social Work.

Krishna Murthy and Others (1992), *Evaluation of the Total Literacy Campaign, Chittoor District, A Report*, Hyderabad: The University of Hyderabad.

Michale Tharakan (1990), *The Ernakulam District Total Literacy Programme*, Report of Evaluation, Trivandrum: Centre for Development Studies.

Ministry of Human Resource Development, (1986), *New Education Policy 1986: Programme of Action*, New Delhi: Govt. of India.

Mohanty and Prusty (1996), "A Study of the Problems of Functioning of 'Jana Shikshana Nilayams" *Indian Journal of Adult Education*, Vol. 57 (2), April-June, pp. 46-51.

Mustaq Ahamad (1992), *An Evaluation on Total Literacy Campaign of Midnapur District (West Bengal)*, New Delhi: NLM Authority.

Mustaq Ahmad (1994), *Evaluation of Literacy Campaign Almora*, Lucknow: State Resource Centre.

Muthuchamy (1992), *A Study of the Role Performance of the Preraks*. M.Phil. Dissertation, Alagappa University.

Nair, Omanna and Rahim (1992), *A Study of the Programmes and Activities of JSN Organised* by Nehru Yuva Kendra in Kerala. Trivendrum: Kerala Association for Non-formal Education and Development.

On Mehta and others (1994), *Evaluation of Literacy Campaign Durg District*, cited in *Evaluation of Literacy Campaigns: Summary Report*, New Delhi: Govt. of India.

Padmanabaiah and Kumarswamy (1995), "An Identification of the Problems Faced by the Monitors", *Indian Journal of Adult Education*, Vol. 50 (2), April-June, pp. 42-46.

Paul Valiakanadathil and Savavanan (1993), *Evaluation of Literacy Campaign, Mandya District*, Bangalore: Indian Social Science Institute.

Reddeppa (1993), *A Study of the Determinants of Prerak Effectiveness*, M.Phil. Thesis, S.V. University.

Sardar Patel Institute of Economic and Social Research (1994), *Evaluation of Literacy Campaign of Dang District*, Ahmedabad: SPIESR.

Sardar Patel Institute of Economic and Social Research (1994), *Evaluation of Literacy Campaign Sunder Nagar District*, Ahmedabad: SPIESR.

Sardar Patel Institute of Economics and Social Research (1993), *Evaluation of Literacy Campaign Bhav Nagar City*, Ahmedabad: SPIESR.

Sardar Patel Institute of Economic and Social Research (1993), *Evaluation of Literacy Campaign Ahmedabad Rural*, Ahmedabad: SPIESR.

Sardar Patel Institute of Economic and Social Research (1993), *Evaluation of Literacy Campaign*, Kheda District, Ahmadabad: SPIESR.

Shanta Mohan (1994), *Evaluation of Literacy Campaign : Dakshina Kannada*, Bangalore: Institute of Social and Economic Change.

Shastri and Chariyulu (1993), *Evaluation of Literacy Campaign. West Godavari District*, Hyderabad: NIRD.

Shukla, A.N. (1972), The Concept of Extension Education: Study in Psychophysical Methods in PRS. Sinha (Ed.) *Studies in Extension*

Education, Hyderabad: National Institute of Community Development.

Sidda Gowda (1996), *Akshara Vani, External Evaluation Report of Total Literacy Campaign, Chitradurga District*, Karnataka, Mysore: Mysore University.

State Resource Centre (1995), *An Observational Study to Identify the Role of JSN in Continuing Education, Mysore:* SRC.

Tata Institute of Social Sciences (1993), *Evaluation of Literacy Campaign Pune Rural*, Bombay: TISS.

Tata Institute of Social Sciences (1993), *Evaluation of Literacy Campaign*, Nanded, Bombay: TISS.

Tata Institute of Social Sciences (1993), *Evaluation of Literacy Campaign*, Latur, Bombay: TISS.

Tribal and Harijan Research cum Training Institute (1993), *Evaluation of Literacy Campaign*, Sundergarh, Bhubaneshwar: THRTI.

Vasumathi (1992), A Study of the Organisation and Functions of Jana Shikshana Nilayams under Area Development Approach of the NLM in the Colleges of Kannur Disrict. Master Dissertation, Calicut University.

Appendices

APPENDIX - I

A Scale to Measure the Suitability of the Learning Materials to the ATP Participants

1. Name: 2. Sex:

3. Caste: 4. Age:

5. Level of Education:

6. Experience in Adult Education:

A few items meant to measure ATP functionaries attitude towards suitability of learning materials for the children used in ATP were given below. Kindly go through all the items and indicate your opinion by ticking one of the 5 alternatives given against each item. The five alternative cues given are fully disagree (1), disagree (2), neutral (3), agree (4) and fully agree (5).

1.	Contents of the primers are also relevant to children.	1 2 3 4 5
2.	Contents were not arranged in alphabetical order.	1 2 3 4 5
3.	Unused words by children incorporated in the primers.	1 2 3 4 5
4.	Free slate and slate pencil might have motivated the children.	1 2 3 4 5
5.	Signs of vowels were not introduced in order.	1 2 3 4 5

6. In filling the blanks of words, it is always better for the children to leave a blank at the ends of the word than at the beginning of words. 1 2 3 4 5
7. Even the functionaries do not know the meanings of some of the words. 1 2 3 4 5
8. Sentences should be smaller. 1 2 3 4 5
9. There are no proper instructions for exercises. 1 2 3 4 5
10. The words used are not suitable to all ages. 1 2 3 4 5
11. The pictures are not attractive to the children. 1 2 3 4 5
12. There is no relevance between pictures and contents. 1 2 3 4 5
13. The contents of the books are not promoting childrens interest in learning. 1 2 3 4 5
14. The childrens are not able to read the PL4 book indenpendently. 1 2 3 4 5
15. The names of the lessons are not meaningfully coined. 1 2 3 4 5
16. There is no relevance between the content and headings of the lessons. 1 2 3 4 5
17. The titles of the chapters should not be lengthy. 1 2 3 4 5
18. Some of the words are giving more than one meaning. 1 2 3 4 5
19. Some of the words are not relevant to the day to day life of children. 1 2 3 4 5
20. Difficult words are used in the primers. 1 2 3 4 5
21. Most of the chapters are related to the children. 1 2 3 4 5
22. Unwanted words are used. 1 2 3 4 5
23. The contents are not relevant to the interests of the children. 1 2 3 4 5
24. There is no relevance between contents and real life situation. 1 2 3 4 5

25. The learning material possess many new items to be learnt. 1 2 3 4 5
26. It is impossible to complete the materials within stipulated time by the children. 1 2 3 4 5
27. Very few children related issues were incorporated in the materials. 1 2 3 4 5
28. Only a few developmental aspects were relevant to the children incorporated in the materials. 1 2 3 4 5
29. Awareness aspects incorporated in the primers are not relevant to the children. 1 2 3 4 5
30. The learning materials were not capable of imporving the pace of learning among the children. 1 2 3 4 5
31. The new methods of teaching is not suitable to the children. 1 2 3 4 5
32. Numeracy was not given prominence in the learning materials. 1 2 3 4 5
33. Most of the contents in the primers are of abstract in nature. 1 2 3 4 5
34. The standard of language used in the primers is high. 1 2 3 4 5
35. To sentence formation is not appropriate to the age of the children. 1 2 3 4 5
36. Sufficient importance for knowledge items in the primers. 1 2 3 4 5
37. Suitable learning exercises are not suitable to the children. 1 2 3 4 5
38. The opening sentences in the chapters are thought provoking. 1 2 3 4 5
39. Concluding paras of the chapters are not thought provoking. 1 2 3 4 5
40. Interest of the children could not be sustained due to bulkiness of the primers. 1 2 3 4 5

41.	Award of certificates for promoting interest among the children.	1 2 3 4 5
42.	Functionaries were not given proper instructions to deal with the numerical exercise relevant to the children.	1 2 3 4 5
43.	The functionaries were not given adequate directions about the methods of using primers suitable to the children.	1 2 3 4 5

APPENDIX-II

An Attitude Scale to Measure Voluteer's Attitudes Towards Akshara Thapasman Programme of Chittoor District

The attitude of the volunteers towards the Akshara Thapasman Programme, may not be uniform. Hence in order to measure the attitude of the volunteer a few attitudinal items are given below. Kindly go through the items and indicate your opinion by ticking one of the alternatives. The five alternative are fully disagree (1), disagree (2), neutral (3), agree (4) and fully agree (5) are given.

A. Personla Information

1.	Name	2.	Sex	3.	Age
4.	Caste	5.	Income	6.	Occupation
7.	Education	8.	Experience in AE		
9.	Marital Status				

B. Attitudinal Items

1.	Propagation about the Total Literacy Campaign in rural areas is not satisfactory.	1 2 3 4 5
2.	The literacy propagation has not reached the target.	1 2 3 4 5
3.	The duration of the Training is inadequate.	1 2 3 4 5
4.	Very few items were covered during Training Programmes.	1 2 3 4 5
5.	Inadequate coverage of the usage of teaching-learning materials during training programme.	1 2 3 4 5
6.	The training programme is above the level of functionaries.	1 2 3 4 5
7.	Untimely supply of teaching learning materials.	1 2 3 4 5
8.	The contents of the primers are suitable to the learners.	1 2 3 4 5
9.	The contents of the primers were not arranged logically order.	1 2 3 4 5
10.	The timing of the ATP centres are not suitable to the learners.	1 2 3 4 5

11.	Financial difficulties are the major causes for arranging extension lectures at the centre.	1 2 3 4 5
12.	Investment in literacy is a waste as per the opinion of the people.	1 2 3 4 5
13.	Illiterates have participated effectively in the programme.	1 2 3 4 5
14.	The volunteers are not adequately motivated due to lack incentives.	1 2 3 4 5
15.	The functionaries participation in the programme is inadequate due to lack of recognition and incentives.	1 2 3 4 5
16.	There is inadequate cooperation from the local leaders for the programme.	1 2 3 4 5
17.	The village leaders and land lords have discouraged the participation of learners as they may lose their grip over the villages.	1 2 3 4 5
18.	High dropout rate is also responsible for failure of the programme.	1 2 3 4 5
19.	The educated youth in the village have not supported the programme whole heatedly.	1 2 3 4 5
20.	The new method of learning made the learners feel difficult to learn.	1 2 3 4 5
21.	Due to new method of teaching and functionaries could not cope up.	1 2 3 4 5
22.	The participation of functionaries is effective though there is no honorarium.	1 2 3 4 5
23.	There are no guidelines for effective supervision of functionaries.	1 2 3 4 5
24.	It is difficult to inform the officials about the progress of programme.	1 2 3 4 5
25.	There is delay in informing the district officials about field problems.	1 2 3 4 5
26.	The assistance of the area coordinator is not available in time.	1 2 3 4 5

27. The assistance from higher official for the development of the programme is not available. 1 2 3 4 5
28. There is no cooperation from the officials of the developmental department for the promotion of the programme. 1 2 3 4 5
29. The officials did not keep up the promises made at the beginning of the programme. 1 2 3 4 5
30. The Higher Officials does not have an understanding about the field problems. 1 2 3 4 5
31. Teacher's participation in the programme is due to the pressure of higher officials. 1 2 3 4 5
32. Field functionaries performed their duties only due to pressure of the higher officials. 1 2 3 4 5
33. The local employees have assisted the programme effectively. 1 2 3 4 5
34. Teachers participating in the programme are not doing justice to their jobs in schools. 1 2 3 4 5
35. The people are of the opinion that the programme is not useful. 1 2 3 4 5
36. The official does not have control over field functionaries due to their voluntary participation. 1 2 3 4 5
37. The target group does not have favourable attitude and understanding of the programme. 1 2 3 4 5
38. If the illiterates understand the importance of education, they will voluntarily participate in the programme. 1 2 3 4 5
39. The programme could not be organised effectively in view of the failure of keeping the promises by the officials. 1 2 3 4 5
40. The volunteers and monitors might have performed their duties effectively if they were paid some honorarium. 1 2 3 4 5

41. Small incentives to the learner will improve their participation. 1 2 3 4 5
42. The programme could not be organised effectively due to the socio-economic variations between learners and functionaries. 1 2 3 4 5
43. The programme was not successful in villages due to bad habits of the parents. 1 2 3 4 5

APPENDIX-III

Questionnaire to Measure The Performance of JCK

I. Information about Monitor

(*a*) Name:

(*b*) Sex: Male/Female

(*c*) Caste: SC/ST. B. C, O.C

(*d*) Occupation:

(*e*) Income:

(*f*) Experience in A.E.:

(*g*) Educational Qualification:

(*h*) Marital Status: Married/Unmarried.

II. Information about JCK

1. Normally at what time the JCK activities will be held?

   (*a*) Morning (*b*) Afternoon (*c*) Evening (*d*) Night.

2. Specify the timing of JCK

   (*a*) Morning from ________ to ________

   (*b*) Afternoon from ________ to ________

   (*c*) Evening from ________ to ________

   (*d*) Night from ________ to ________

3. Place of conducting the JCK

   (*a*) School (*b*) Temple (*c*) Panchayath office
   (*d*) Village meeting place (*e*) Monitor house (f)________.

4. Lighting facilities available at JCK

   (*a*) Petromax light (*b*) Kerosine Lamp (*c*) Electricity.

5. The type of accommodation available to JCK

   (*a*) Hut (*b*) Kutcha House (*c*) Daba House
   (*d*) Packa House (*e*) Others.

III Organisation of Library

6. The facilities available in JCK Library.

   (a) Special room *(b)* Steel Almara *(c)* Table *(d)* Chair

   (e) Mats *(f)* Lights *(g)* Fans *(h)* Benches (*i*) Others.

7. At what time the adults attending the JCK Library.

   (a) Morning *(b)* Afternoon *(c)* Evening *(d)* Night.

8. Generally who are all the people coming to he JCK Library.

   (a) Neo-literates *(b)* Drop outs *(c)* Adults

   (d) Non-formal Education Learners *(e)* others.

9. Of the above who visits the library frequently.

   A B C D E

   (Please mark the number specified above).

10. Who attend the JCK Library frequently?

    (a) Male *(b)* Female.

11. Specify the facilities available in JCK Library for keeping the books.

    Ans:

12. What are the facilities available for circulating the books in other villages.

13. How far the villagers utilising the books in N JCK library.

    (a) Very effectively *(b)* Effectively *(c)* Moderately

    (d) Less effectively *(e)* Very less effectively.

14. How far the books available in JCK Library are relevant to the peoples interest.

    (a) Highly relevant *(b)* Relevant *(c)* Moderately

    (d) In a limited way *(e)* Not so relevant.

15. To what extend the villages are cooperating for organising JCK Library.

    (a) Greater extent *(b)* Great extent *(c)* Certain extent

    (d) Limited extent *(e)* Very limited extent.

16. The what extent the people are returning the books to JCK Library.

    (a) Less than 25 per cent *(b)* 26 to 50 per cent

    (c) 51 to 75 per cent *(d)* 76 to 100 per cent.

17. Have your provided any additional facilities to JCK Library.

    Ans:

18. Whether the JCK is receiving News papers regularly Yes/No (If no specify the reason).

19. Specify the magazines supplied to the JCK.

IV Organisation of Chercha Mandal

20. Do you organise chercha mandal in JCK?

21. Generally How many times you are organising chercha mandal per month.

    Ans:

22. Specify the aspects on which you have organised chercha mandals.

23. Have you provided any facilities for organisation of chercha mandals in JCK.

    Ans:

24. Have you taken any decisions in chercha mandal to solve the problems of villagers.

    Yes/No.

25. If yes how far the decisions taken in chercha mandal are being implemented.

    (a) To a greater extent *(b)* To great extent *(c)* Certain extent *(d)* Limited extent *(e)* Very limited extent.

26. Have you organised special chercha mandal for women.

    Yes/No

27. How far village people participated in the organisation of chercha mandal.

    (a) To a larger extent (b) Large extent *(c)* Certain extent (d) Limited way (e) Very limited way

28. How for the village people co-operated to implement the decision of chercha mandal.

    (a) To a greater extent *(b)* Great extent *(c)* Certain extend

    (d) Limited extent *(e)* Very limited extent.

V Organisation of Short-term Training Programmes

29. Are you organising short term training programmes in JCK

    Yes/No

30. Specify the subjects on aspects which you have arranged lectures from different developmental department experts.

    (a) Health *(b)* Family Welfare *(c)* Agriculture

    (d) Animal husbandry *(e)* Sericulture *(f)* Handicrafts

    (g) Others.

31. Are there any resource persons at your village to inform the latest developments.

    Yes/ No.

32. If yes specify the resource person specialisation.

33. To what extent the above experts co-operate with JCK activities.

(a) Greater extent *(b)* Great extent *(c)* Moderate
(d) Limited extent *(e)* Very limited extent.

34. As a part of JCK activities have you taken the village people to any developmental organisation or project

Yes/No.

35. Where do you get the information on developmental programmes.

    (a) Developmental departments *(b)* Banks
    (c) Voluntary organisation *(d)* Business people
    (e) Social workers *(f)* Others.

36. To what extent the above information useful to the community.

    (a) To a greater extent *(b)* great extent *(c)* certain extent
    (d) Limited extent *(e)* Very limited extent.

VI Organisation of Sports and Games

37. Have you organised sports/ games in JCK

    Yes/No.

38. If yes, specify he facilities available in JCK to organise such sports and games.

    Ans:

39. Name the sports and games material available in JCK

    Ans:

40. What is the extent of utilisation of the sports games material in JCK

    (a) To a greater extent *(b)* greater extent
    (c) Certain extent *(d)* Limited extent
    (e) Very Limited extent.

41. What are all the games and sports in which women have participated.

    Ans:

42. If participated specify the extent of their participation.

    (a) Very Limited *(b)* Limited *(c)* Certain extent
    (d) Great extent *(e)* To a greater extent.

VI Organisation of Recreational and Cultural Activities

43. Have you organised recreational activities in JCK.

    Yes/No

44. If yes specify the activities.

45. To what extent the community participated in recreational activities.

    (a) To a greater extent *(b)* great extent *(c)* certain extent

    (d) limited manner *(e)* Very limited manner.

VII Information Window

46. Do you have T.V. and Radio in your JCK

    Yes/No.

47. If yes, specify.

48. If no have you utilised the T.V. and Radio of the community for JCK activities.

    Yes/No

49. What are the activities undertaken for propagation of JCK activities.

    Ans:

50. How far you have organised the programmes highlighting the utility of literacy Programmes among the community.

    (a) Very limited extent *(b)* Limited extent

    (c) Certain extent *(d)* great extent

    (e) to a greater extent.

APPENDIX-IV

A Scale to Identify the Problems of the Monitors

The preraks has to interact with different groups of people with different back groups while organising JSNs activities and is expected to satisfy the needs of the community. In view of this Prerak has of face a number of problems in discharging his duties. A list of such identified problems are given below. Please go through each problem and identify the problem that you are exposed in discharging your duties. For identifying the intensity of the problem 5 alternative cues are also given i.e.,

1. Very low 2. Low 3. Moderate
4. High 5. Very high.

1.	The time scheduled fixed for JSN by the Govt. is sufficient.	1 2 3 4 5
2.	The honorarium paid to the Prerak is very low.	1 2 3 4 5
3.	The preraks need not be recognised as other social workers.	1 2 3 4 5
4.	The personal works of the preraks are obsticals to JSN activities.	1 2 3 4 5
5.	Village politics are affecting the JSN activities.	1 2 3 4 5
6.	Getting co-operation from village elders for JSN activities is difficult.	1 2 3 4 5
7.	The training received by the Prerak is not useful for the Prerak in organising JSN activities.	1 2 3 4 5
8.	Lack of Cooperation from programme administrators in organizing JSN activities.	1 2 3 4 5
9.	The time allocated for organising literacy centre in JSN is not sufficient.	1 2 3 4 5
10.	Lack of interest for promotion of literacy among the neo-literates.	1 2 3 4 5

11.	Too much participation of village educated in JSN activities is becoming an obstacle for continuing education of neo-literates.	1 2 3 4 5
12.	Lack of adequate facilities for JSN Library.	1 2 3 4 5
13.	Community participation in chercha Mandal is inadequate.	1 2 3 4 5
14.	The chercha Mandal activities are not useful to the villagers.	1 2 3 4 5
15.	Organising games and sports in JSN is very difficult.	1 2 3 4 5
16.	The developmental departments are not helpful in JSN activities.	1 2 3 4 5
17.	The JSN is not able to met the requirements of the villages.	1 2 3 4 5

APPENDIX-V

Community Attitude Scale

In order to identify the attitude of the community towards various aspects of JCK some items were given below. Kindly go through them. In order to mark your attitude five alternatives viz. Fully agree (5), Agree (4) Undecided (3), Disagree (2), Fully disagree (1), is given, Check all the items.

1.	The books available in JCK are relevant to the interests of the community.	1 2 3 4 5
2.	Books borrowed from the library should be returned in time.	1 2 3 4 5
3.	The JCK is not receiving the Magazines in time.	1 2 3 4 5
4.	The books in the JCK library are readily available for the community.	1 2 3 4 5
5.	Churcha mandals are not organised in JCK.	1 2 3 4 5
6.	The JCK activities are affected due to village politics.	1 2 3 4 5
7.	Community people is able to spend the time fruitfully due to JCK activities.	1 2 3 4 5
8.	The implementation of churcha mandal decisions are not so useful for the village development.	1 2 3 4 5
9.	The organisation of inter village sports and games are promoting integration among different sections of the people in the villages.	1 2 3 4 5
10.	The men and women were not able to participate equally in JCK activities due to traditions and customs.	1 2 3 4 5
11.	The participation of villagers is more in case of entertainment programmes.	1 2 3 4 5
12.	The games and sports material available in the JCK is not suitable to the villagers.	1 2 3 4 5

13. The Monitor is not capable of promoting the participation of women in games and sports. 1 2 3 4 5

14. The literacy centre organised by the JCK is not up to the mark. 1 2 3 4 5

15. Location of JCK is suitable to all the people in the community. 1 2 3 4 5

16. Monitor is capable of promoting unity among different sections of the people. 1 2 3 4 5

17. The extension lectures organised by JCK are more useful to the community. 1 2 3 4 5

18. The timings of the JCK is not suitable to all. 1 2 3 4 5

19. The JCK is not having minimum infrastructive facilities for its activities. 1 2 3 4 5

20. Lack of T.V. Radio, Tape recorder is a big handicap for successful implementation of JCK activities. 1 2 3 4 5

APPENDIX-VI

JCK Community Support Scale

A few items relating to the community support towards JCK activities are given below. Kindly go through the items and identify to what extent you have supported the JCK activities. In order to identify your support 5 alternatives cues were given Viz. Strongly supported (5), Supported (4), Neutral (3), Not supported (2), Not at all supported (1), You can choose any one of the alternative cues for representing your support.

1. Identifying suitable place for locating JCK. 1 2 3 4 5
2. Village level literacy committee members fully cooperating with JCK activities. 1 2 3 4 5
3. Community has contributed the materials required for JCK activities. 1 2 3 4 5
4. Community has liberally donates the reading material to the JCK library. 1 2 3 4 5
5. The community is returning the books in time from JCK Library. 1 2 3 4 5
6. Irrespective of political divisions all sections of the community is participating in JCK churcha mandal. 1 2 3 4 5
7. The villagers are spending their leisure time fruitfully through JCK activities. 1 2 3 4 5
8. The villagers are implementing the decisions taken by the churcha mandal. 1 2 3 4 5
9. Community participation is less in village development activities. 1 2 3 4 5
10. Lack of community participation in Inter village sports and games. 1 2 3 4 5
11. Lack of Co-operation from villagers in encouraging the women to participate in JCK activities. 1 2 3 4 5

12. Community is supporting in organisation of recreational programmes. 1 2 3 4 5
13. Community is not coming forward to utilise the games and sports material available at JCK. 1 2 3 4 5
14. Women is not effectively participating in games and sports. 1 2 3 4 5
15. Community is effectively utilising the extension lectures organised by the JCKs. 1 2 3 4 5
16. Literacy centre is fully utilised by the community. 1 2 3 4 5
17. Community is contributing material support for organisation of recreational programmes at JCKs. 1 2 3 4 5

APPENDIX-VII

A Scale to Measure the ATP Functionaries Attitude Towards Effectiveness of Training, Monitoring and Evaluation

In order to identify your attitude towards the effectiveness of the Training, Monitoring & Evaluation Procedures adopted in the ATP, a few statements are given below. Read the items and indicate whether you strongly agree (1), agree (2), undecided (3), disagree (4), and strongly disagree (5), with each of the statement.

A. Training

1.	The duration of the Training Schedule for the field functionaries is sufficient.	1 2 3 4 5
2.	Only important aspects should be given priority in the Training Programme.	1 2 3 4 5
3.	Sufficient time and priority were not allocated to aspects relating to teaching methods.	1 2 3 4 5
4.	The training was not successful due to lack of sufficient interaction between participating and resource persons.	1 2 3 4 5
5.	Training Programme could not attract the attention of the participants inview of wide usage of lecture method.	1 2 3 4 5
6.	Sufficient training was not given in utilisation of locally available resources for the benefit of the ATP.	1 2 3 4 5
7.	Sufficient attention was not given to the methods of effective utilisation of teaching learning materials.	1 2 3 4 5
8.	It would have been better if the training programme was evaluated immediately after its completion.	1 2 3 4 5
9.	The curriculum of the training should have been formulated based on the understanding of functionaries about the programme.	1 2 3 4 5

10. Experts of the Development Departments should have been involved for effective training. 1 2 3 4 5

11. Training study materials were not provided during the training programme. 1 2 3 4 5

12. The organisation of follow-up training will improve the effectiveness of the functionaries. 1 2 3 4 5

13. Sufficient training was not given for maintaining the records. 1 2 3 4 5

B. Monitoring and Evaluation

1. The progress reports sheet ment for monitoring the progress was not upto mark. 1 2 3 4 5

2. The supervision of the higher officials to the field is not yielding desired results. 1 2 3 4 5

3. The filling the progress reports is consuming more time. 1 2 3 4 5

4. The participants were not able to complete the primers in the prescribed period. 1 2 3 4 5

5. The Summative Evaluation of the learners is only nominal. 1 2 3 4 5

6. Apart from literacy, the components of social awareness should have been incorporated in the achievement test. 1 2 3 4 5

7. Evaluation has done for its own sake but not aimed to assess the performance of the participants. 1 2 3 4 5

8. The inbuilt evaluation in the primers is not serving the purpose. 1 2 3 4 5

9. The evaluation was not aimed to study the impact of literacy on the participants day to day life. 1 2 3 4 5

10. The monitoring is less effective in view of lack of co-ordination among the programme functionaries. 1 2 3 4 5

APPENDIX-VIII

A Scale to Measure Monitor Effectiveness

Monitor require certain skills to organise the activities of JCK. Some of the items relating to such skills are given below. Please go through the items clearly. Appraise yourself with regard to your performance of the items, and mention your level of performance. To mention your level of performance 5 levels of performance were given below— Very difficult (1), Difficult (2), Moderate (3), Easy (4) and Very easy (5).

1.	Conducting JCK activities leading to the strengthening of literacy and awareness the neo-literates.	1 2 3 4 5
2.	Collecting and maintaining the need-based materials for neo-literates at the JCK.	1 2 3 4 5
3.	The needed study material must be collected and kept in JCK for favour of the learners.	1 2 3 4 5
4.	Solving the problems of villagers in the chercha mandal through discussions.	1 2 3 4 5
5.	Conducting short-term vocational training programmes.	1 2 3 4 5
6.	Conducting inter-village sports and games.	1 2 3 4 5
7.	Conducting entertainment and cultural programmes.	1 2 3 4 5
8.	Collecting required books and newspapers voluntarily.	1 2 3 4 5
9.	Execution of JCK programmes in the jurisdiction of JCK village.	1 2 3 4 5
10.	Selection a suitable place for conducting JCK activities.	1 2 3 4 5
11.	Conducting JCK programmes rising above the village politics.	1 2 3 4 5
12.	Attracting the villagers through JCK programmes.	1 2 3 4 5

13. Getting help from Government officials for carrying out the JCK programmes. 1 2 3 4 5
14. Framing post-literacy programmes for the neo-literates. 1 2 3 4 5
15. Distribution of books for all villages in the jurisdiction of JCK. 1 2 3 4 5
16. Organising extension lectures by officials regarding the developmental programmes. 1 2 3 4 5
17. Supervising the Adult education centres. 1 2 3 4 5
18. Supervising the Non-formal education centres under the JCK jurisdiction. 1 2 3 4 5
19. Making good use of audiovisual equipment while teaching. 1 2 3 4 5
20. Imparting the health principles to the villages, with the help of the doctors. 1 2 3 4 5
21. Conducting separate Chercha mandal for women. 1 2 3 4 5
22. Sending the reports in time about the JCK programmes to the higher officials. 1 2 3 4 5
23. Bringing the problems of the villagers to the notice of the concerned officials and solving them. 1 2 3 4 5
24. Conducting the advisory committee meeting in JCK. 1 2 3 4 5
25. Taking the help of the people in conducting JCK programmes. 1 2 3 4 5
26. Taking steps to implement the developmental programmes in the villages. 1 2 3 4 5
27. Helping the voluntary organisations in their activities. 1 2 3 4 5
28. Motivating the youth to participate in the developmental programmes in the village. 1 2 3 4 5

29.	Collecting and preserving the social, economic cultural inormation of the village.	1 2 3 4 5
30.	Making the learners to understand their progress in occupational skills.	1 2 3 4 5
31.	Promoting the good habits among the neo-literates.	1 2 3 4 5
32.	Giving training to the adults for the effective use of their leisure time.	1 2 3 4 5
33.	Conducting tests to know the progress of learning among adults.	1 2 3 4 5
34.	Developing the skills to solve the problems of the neo-literates by themselves in JCK.	1 2 3 4 5
35.	Giving special training for the slow learners.	1 2 3 4 5
36.	Proper maintenance of all registers in the JCK.	1 2 3 4 5
37.	To make full use of the skills and service of the villagers in JCK programmes.	1 2 3 4 5
38.	Eradicating superstitious beliefs and untouchability in the society.	1 2 3 4 5
39.	Keeping the adults away from bad habits.	1 2 3 4 5
40.	Encouraging the new learners for their further studies.	1 2 3 4 5
41.	Conducting JCK programmes according to the needs and necessity of the villagers.	1 2 3 4 5
42.	Making the villages and the elders of the village to participate in the JCK programmes.	1 2 3 4 5
43.	Conducting educational entertainment and excursions for the benefit of the villagers.	1 2 3 4 5
44.	Creating awareness about the important national day celebrations.	1 2 3 4 5
45.	Developing unity and integrity among the people of the village by removing the existing differences between them.	1 2 3 4 5

21. Along with literacy, real life situation examples are utilised for the promotion of arithmetics. 1 2 3 4 5

22. Utility of TV and radio in JCK motivates the neo-literates to make efforts in retention of literacy. 1 2 3 4 5

23. The utility of day to day experiences are better than the scientific methods in retention of literacy activities. 1 2 3 4 5

24. The JCK is giving more importance for social awareness than literacy components in the activities relating to retention of literacy. 1 2 3 4 5

Index